TEACHING
with LIGHT

"Give light and people will find the way."

—Ella Baker

TEACHING
with LIGHT

TEN LESSONS FOR FINDING WISDOM, BALANCE, & INSPIRATION

CAROL PELLETIER RADFORD

FOREWORD BY
KRISTEN LEE

FOR INFORMATION:

Corwin
A SAGE Company
2455 Teller Road
Thousand Oaks, California 91320
(800) 233-9936
www.corwin.com

SAGE Publications Ltd.
1 Oliver's Yard
55 City Road
London EC1Y 1SP
United Kingdom

SAGE Publications India Pvt. Ltd.
B 1/I 1 Mohan Cooperative Industrial Area
Mathura Road, New Delhi 110 044
India

SAGE Publications Asia-Pacific Pte. Ltd.
18 Cross Street #10-10/11/12
China Square Central
Singapore 048423

Acquisitions Editor: Eliza B. Erickson
Project Editor: Amy Schroller
Copy Editor: Deanna Noga
Typesetter: C&M Digitals (P) Ltd.
Proofreader: Rae-Ann Goodwin
Cover Designer: Scott Van Atta
Marketing Manager: Margaret O'Connor

Printed in the United States of America

Library of Congress Cataloging-in-Publication Data

Names: Radford, Carol Pelletier, author.

Title: Teaching with light : ten lessons for finding wisdom, balance, and inspiration / Carol Pelletier Radford.

Description: Thousand Oaks, California : Corwin, 2021. | Includes bibliographical references.

Identifiers: LCCN 2020052559 | ISBN 9781071822708 (paperback) | ISBN 9781071822692 (epub) | ISBN 9781071822685 (epub) | ISBN 9781071822678 (pdf)

Subjects: LCSH: Teaching—Pyschological aspects. | Teachers—Job satisfaction—United States. | Teacher morale—United States. | Teacher turnover—United States—Prevention.

Classification: LCC LB2840 .R328 2021 | DDC 371.1001/9—dc23
LC record available at https://lccn.loc.gov/2020052559

This book is printed on acid-free paper.

21 22 23 24 25 10 9 8 7 6 5 4 3 2 1

CONTENTS

Visit the companion website at
resources.corwin.com/TeachingWithLight
for additional resources and downloadable materials.

FOREWORD

Nowadays, it's unusual for the phone to ring, unless something is wrong. I found it odd that my phone was ringing—especially on a Sunday night after dinner, one of those rare, reliably quiet moments of my week.

I almost let it go to voice mail, but wasn't sure if it was a patient in distress, and I was willing to take the chance that I could maneuver away from a telemarketer if that's what the situation called for.

It ended up being a call that would change not only the course of my teaching, but also my life.

I was greeted by a gregarious spirit with a Massachusetts accent. I'm pretty sure she said her name was Carol, but she's talking fast, so I couldn't be sure. She got right down to it: She was a teacher who teaches teachers, and she was worried about all the stress they're under. She wanted to know if I would run one of my teacher stress workshops where she directed programming at the Center for School and University Partnerships in our community to help new teachers. She had stumbled across a brochure showcasing my work on educator well-being and felt that my clinical expertise with teachers would be beneficial. We talked about the risks teachers face in education and how little training is devoted to providing evidence-based tools to help them flourish. We bantered back and forth about our grave concerns for teachers and what we believed needed to happen to make it better. I'd been working as a psychotherapist with teachers experiencing burnout in clinical settings. The same themes I was seeing in the therapy room were the same in her classroom. Carol's enthusiasm and deep intellect was not lost on me. I looked at the clock. What felt like five seconds turned out to be 50 minutes. I was sold.

Before we hung up, I asked her to repeat her full name slower: Carol. Pelletier. Radford. We said goodbye and the yellow sticky note I'd scratched her name down onto alerted me: *C.P.R . . .* her initials are "*CPR*"!

The significance of her initials soon became real to me when I met Carol. It was just like our phone call; she was real. She walks the talk; she breathes air into everyone she meets; and she is smart and wise beyond compare—without a whiff of pretentiousness or arrogance. I am not being overdramatic when I say that her picture should be listed under "light" in *Webster's*. It is no surprise that this book is titled *Teaching With Light*—it's exactly what Carol lives and breathes in and out. It's like Lady Gaga writing a book on performing. *Light* is *signature Carol*—and her track record as an educator and thought leader in teaching and mentoring reflects this.

Carol holds a Harvard doctorate, is an award-winning educator, best-selling author with a 40-year legacy in education, and indomitable spirit. Her work has touched tens of thousands across the world. She is a true sage and agent of change—one who wants to share her wisdom and passion to help all educators find our way during increasingly complex circumstances. Carol *is* the Pied-Piper: savvy, brilliant, approachable, and fun to be around. Her energy is contagious; it will not take you long to feel her unique flare as you dig into this book.

It's hard to pry Carol's many accomplishments out of her. Years after our first encounter, over a glass of wine and cheesecake, I remember trying to get her to open up about her book sales and such. She was intentionally vague and clearly squirmy. This was the last of her concerns. Those metrics were insignificant and underwhelming to Carol—she does what she does because she loves it; she knows the difference it makes.

This book isn't prescriptive, tone deaf of what teachers *actually face*, or oversimplified. It is deeply rooted within a legacy of teaching and helping teachers reflect on their purpose, stay the course, and remain inspired despite the very real struggles we all face. Carol masterfully lays out ways we can rediscover our intentions and teach, lead, and live in values-aligned ways. She reminds us to tune in to our stories and the *why* of our work. She provides solid strategies on self-care, ones that can not only illuminate our own pathways to flourish, but also serve as beacons within our own learning ecosystems.

Beyond her expertise in traditional education, Carol is a certified yoga teacher and mindfulness extraordinaire. The upper level of her home is filled with beautiful artwork she's created, ranging from portraits made out of blue-green sea glass from her family in Italy, to waves that embody her residences on Cape Cod and Venice, Florida. She's made journals, calendars, and cards, which all, like the artwork in this book, represent her glowing aura and tremendous commitment to living a heart-led life, and inspiring us all to do the same. I am not generally a fan of commenting on a way that a woman dresses, but Carol's sense of style, which she's known for, is another embodiment of her creativity, pizazz, and boisterous soul. She is an *educator-artist*.

It has been 10 years since the infamous Sunday night call. She is now saved on my iPhone as *Carol Mama Mentor*. After the work at the university, Carol has remained a beacon for me through my dissertation on urban teacher burnout, in the early stages of my teaching career, the writing of my first two books, my first research paper presentation in Santa Fe, New Mexico, and all the professional and personal twists and turns a life can take in a decade. I cannot think of a greater influence on my work and my life than Carol Pelletier Radford.

At a time when teachers are facing unthinkable strains, this book could not be timelier. My hope is that every page will provide you the right dose of *CPR* and remind you of the sacredness of your work and life. Carol shows us in this book and in the manner she lives her life that we too can be beacons of light, even during dark times.

Like all of Carol's work and ways of engaging in life, *Teaching With Light* provides a healthy dose of practical wisdom and divine inspiration. What I love most about it is the warmth and enthusiasm of her voice, much like that Sunday night when she first called me. I hope you will answer her call, too.

—Kristen Lee, EdD, LICSW
Lead Faculty, Behavioral Science
Faculty in Residence; Associate Teaching Professor
College of Professional Studies, Northeastern University
Author, *RESET: Make the Most of Your Stress: Your 24-7 Plan for Well-Being*
and *Mentalligence: A New Psychology of Thinking—Learn What It Takes to Be More Agile, Mindful, and Connected in Today's World*

PREFACE

WELCOME LETTER TO THE READERS

Dear Friends,

Teaching With Light reflects the message in Ella Baker's quote at the beginning of this book, "Give light and people will find the way." I believe when we find the light within us and share it with our colleagues, parents, and students, we become powerful influences on the teaching profession. Together, our positive light will brilliantly shine and light the way for us all.

I am writing this book because I have had a long and fulfilling career as a teacher and now it is time to pay it forward. I still love teaching. I taught in an elementary classroom for 21 years and then moved to teacher preparation for 21 more years. After that, I started my own company, and I continue to engage in education-related conversations.

I am still passionate about teaching and feel the spark deep inside that encourages me to share what I have learned with others. I believe we can build on our success stories and learn from our struggles so the next generation of teachers doesn't have to reinvent the wheel. We can build on the wisdom of other teachers when we listen to their stories. We can learn from inspiring and influential leaders when we listen to their messages. This is a book that includes stories of resilience, courage, and optimism. It also includes practical strategies that help us find and maintain our balance through trying times. We need each other, and we need to focus on our well-being. Teachers who are happy and healthy offer their students a model for positive learning and living. As I reflect on my successful career, I have learned many lessons.

> I hope the Ten Lessons I have included in this book help you overcome your day-to-day challenges as an educator and also remind you to focus on the joy that still exists for you in teaching.

The lessons in this book reveal our vulnerabilities as well as our strengths. It is an opportunity to reflect on what is most meaningful in our careers and how we can use this wisdom to support others. My career is filled with many guides and mentors. Examples of their inspiration, advice, and the messages that came to me when I needed them are integrated into the pages of this book.

Living and teaching are connected. What we do in our personal lives influences who we are in the classroom. That is why it is so important for us to understand how to stay healthy physically and emotionally. Self-care, wellness practices, and inspiration from others can help us open up to receive joy and give us opportunities to express gratitude. These practices can also support us in responding to challenges in ways that minimize our hurts and anxieties. I believe teachers are strong and creative. We can rise above the challenges that are put in our path if we teach from our hearts.

Teaching With Light is my legacy offering to teachers. My hope is that you will be inspired to find your story in these Ten Lessons and the wisdom that emerges will illuminate your path ahead.

In gratitude for those who teach,
Carol
Carol Pelletier Radford, EdD
Falmouth, Massachusetts, and Venice, Florida

IN GRATITUDE

There are so many students, so many teachers, so many mentors—too many to name. You know who you are. Some of you will see your name in the book mentioned as a resource or listed as an inspiring leader; others will read my stories or listen to the podcasts and know I am talking about YOU! All of you have touched my heart and soul and given me the gifts of your time, encouragement, and critique.

Special thanks to Corwin for believing in me and seeing the vision for this book. *Teaching With Light* acknowledges that it is the light within us that makes us the teachers we are meant to be.

Thank you all for being willing to serve the greater good. You have kept my light glowing and made me the teacher I am today.

ABOUT THE AUTHOR

Carol Pelletier Radford is the founder of Mentoring in Action, an organization dedicated to the success of novice teachers and their mentors. Carol is an experienced classroom teacher and teacher education administrator. Her best-selling books *Mentoring in Action: Guiding, Sharing, and Reflecting With Novice Teachers* and *The First Years Matter: Becoming an Effective Teacher* are published by Corwin.

Carol received her doctorate from the Harvard Graduate School of Education, where she focused her studies on mentoring and teacher leadership. She is a certified yoga teacher who practices meditation and shares mindfulness strategies with educators through her online courses and website. Her *Teaching With Light* podcast features teacher stories and inspiring leaders. Her next passion project is the creation of a Teacher Legacy Network, where retired teachers can share their wisdom with aspiring teachers.

You can learn more about Carol, find free resources, videos, meditations, courses, and all her books at mentoringinaction.com.

Twitter @MentorinAction

Facebook @MentoringinAction4Teachers

Instagram @cpradford

For my mother, Marian, who saw the teacher in me.

INTRODUCTION

I welcome classroom teachers, parents, administrators, public policy leaders, university professors, and all who consider themselves teachers to read this book. We all play a teaching role within our schools, districts, and the organizations that support teacher development. Former teachers who transition to new roles bring a sense of teacher reality to their work, and this keeps our profession grounded in the day-to-day practices of educators.

This book is organized into three sections.

Section I provides a context for the Ten Lessons through the research that has influenced my thinking and career decisions. It is framed around three questions: (1) Why do people choose to teach? (2) Why do they leave? and (3) What keeps them teaching? I encourage you to read this section to see how it relates to your experience. I believe teacher well-being relates to student success and the ways in which we intentionally take care of ourselves influences our decisions and in turn our teaching practices. The path we choose and our intentions for our career impact our life choices, our students' success, and our profession. We need support to be effective in our classrooms, so finding our personal mentors is crucial to experiencing our joy. I believe we are the ones who can make a difference, and by recognizing our power we can collectively contribute to the success of our professional community.

Section II is the heart of the book. It shares Ten Lessons I learned over the course of my career as a teacher. Most are teacher stories, but many of them intertwine with my personal life. I have had an abundantly creative career filled with many heartwarming memories, yet I have chosen to share the times when I found myself struggling or when I considered taking a risk. I believe that the times we face challenges are when we need the most guidance, and they are also the times we grow the most.

The titles for each of these Ten Lessons are expressions I have repeated to myself throughout my teaching career. Each one was introduced to me along my path when I needed some advice or a push. I understand that my social interactions and emotions contribute to the ways I respond to others, and these expressions have helped me keep my inner light shining so I could stay on my teaching path. I now see these meaningful messages have illuminated my path when I found myself lost in the drama of everyday life. The expressions helped me trust in myself and take that next small step. They continue to guide me and give me great comfort when I am feeling a bit unsettled or uncertain.

The Ten Lessons are a collection of my teaching stories. Some I have told many times and others revealed themselves to me as I was writing this book. Each lesson in organized into three parts: Wisdom Through Stories, Mindful Living Actions, and Inspiration From the Words of Others. There are audio readings of each lesson's opening message and podcast interviews with teachers and leaders throughout each lesson.

Section III culminates the book with ways to reflect on what you learned. You will have an opportunity to Review, Revisit, and Rethink as you look at your big takeaways from each lesson. This is your opportunity to look at your career intention and see if it gives you joy. Finding our way takes courage. Courage to look at our options, courage to change our route, and courage sometimes to stay put. Only you can make that decision. Choosing to teach with light allows us to make choices so that we can share our positive experiences and learn from our struggles. This section of the book will bring all your reflections together and inspire your next steps.

The book's companion website and the appendices offer many practical resources that can be used in your classroom or office. Review the list of authors who have been an inspiration to me and consider choosing a book to read. Print the posters with the Ten Lessons or the Inspiring Quotes and put them in a place that you can see daily either at home or in your classroom. Review the Reading Plans and decide if you will experience this book as a personal journey or if you will choose to share your insights with other teachers. You can access the companion website by visiting **resources.corwin.com/TeachingWithLight**.

WAYS TO USE THIS BOOK

There are many ways to use this book. You can read it cover to cover, or you can skip around and read the lessons that stand out to you. You may notice a particular piece of art that attracts you to read the message and story for that particular lesson. Some of my friends like to know how a book ends so they always read the last part first! You may choose to begin by reading *Lesson 10* to see where this book is heading and review the resources at the very end of the book. You may even decide to listen to the podcasts first. Whatever you do will be right for you.

This book will engage you and invite you to reveal your inner wisdom through your own stories as well as encourage you to listen to the wisdom of others. My purpose is to offer you the time and space to reflect on your personal stories, assess your well-being, and intentionally seek out inspiration. The format includes the written word, abstract art, audio introductions, famous quotations, self-assessments, mindfulness practices, and podcasts, intentionally designed to appeal to a variety of learning styles.

Reflect on your personal stories, assess your well-being, and intentionally seek out inspiration.

When I created each of the original art abstract pastels that you'll see on the chapter opener pages, I didn't know they matched up with each of the Ten Lessons in this book. The colors or the images may capture your attention and lead you to a message that is meant for you. Let the art speak to you. If you see art that calls to you, read that lesson first. Use the art to call forth the wisdom inside you.

Use this book to reflect on your current role to see if it is fulfilling you. If you are seeking new ways to contribute to the profession, you may want to consider a change. Teachers who transition from the classroom to other roles bring their practical and very real wisdom from the classroom with them. Teacher perspectives can not only influence public policy decisions, but they also can bring common sense and relevance to the education organization's programs. Leaving the classroom is not the goal, but recognizing that some teachers' visions will shift acknowledges that we can teach and support students from other roles within the educational community.

Many of my stories in Section II relate to the other roles I took on outside the classroom or in teacher education and now in my own business. In all these roles I felt inspired to contribute and share what I had learned. I loved being in the classroom where I taught for 21 years, but when my heart pulled me to teacher preparation I saw my gifts and talents being used in a creative way to support student teachers and their mentors. It was a difficult decision to leave the classroom, yet I felt an enthusiasm and passion for teacher education that I needed to follow. *Teaching With Light* offers us an opportunity to look within and see where we are finding joy and how we might choose our next steps.

I encourage you to keep a journal or write your reflections in the book so you can revisit your notes when you read Section III. Take some time now to skim the Reading Plans in Appendix B at the end of the book to decide whether you would like to read this book as a personal journey or share this experience with others.

Teaching With Light is designed as an inspirational tool to support you *wherever* you are on your teaching path. It is a book you can return to again and again and use as a resource to guide you when you feel you are straying from your dreams. This is the beginning of your story.

SECTION I

Illuminating
the Path
Ahead

The research and knowledge that guides our educational community is varied and deep. There are many voices that guide public policy, curriculum design, and education reform. When I think about teachers and our profession, three overarching questions always come to mind:

1. Why do people choose to teach?

2. Why do they leave?

3. What keeps them in teaching?

Three authors have helped me understand the complicated responses to each of these questions. I use their work to illustrate my rationale for this book and how our understanding of the context of education can illuminate our path ahead.

IT TAKES WISDOM, BALANCE, AND INSPIRATION TO TEACH

Why do people choose to teach? I always knew I wanted to be a teacher and followed a traditional path through teacher preparation, but other teachers I have talked with came to teaching in different ways. Some are career changers who explored other professions to earn more money and others say that they fell into teaching by accident and found their life fulfilled in the classroom. Parker J. Palmer's book *The Courage to Teach: Exploring the Inner Landscape of a Teacher's Life* (1998) has had a profound influence on me. His authentic, heart-based message verified my reasons for choosing to teach and why I stay. His ability to reach out to all kinds of teachers in all professions and to capture both the joy and the pain of our daily work made me feel part of an honored group. My journey through his book gave me an inside view of my own capacity to do purposeful work and see my own wisdom. His message throughout was, "[g]ood teaching comes from the identity and integrity of the teacher." These words encouraged me to ask others around me to share their stories of why and how they came to find themselves teachers.

I am honored to say I met Parker in person and spent a weekend with him as part of a retreat. The opportunity arose when the dean at the university had a conflict and I was invited to take her place among other university presidents and education leaders. As a former classroom teacher and recently appointed director of practicum programs, you can imagine I was quite intimidated. When I introduced myself and shared my uncertainty about my role in the group, Parker looked into my eyes through to my soul and said, "You are the reason we are here. You represent the teachers we are talking about." He signed my copy of *Courage to Teach* and wrote, *To Carol – With gratitude for* your *courage to teach – and for your great laughter! Many Blessings, Parker Palmer*. This experience was the beginning of my deeper inquiry into how a teacher's identity relates to why they choose to teach.

Why do teachers leave? After the investment of time and money, the agony of state tests, student teaching, course requirements, and licensing hoops, some people *still* leave. I am more interested in the stories teachers tell than the statistics informing me how many teachers leave. I recently reconnected with a woman who graduated from the teacher preparation program I led 20 years ago. I asked how long she taught, and she replied, "One year." I was shocked. She was one of our best student teachers! Her story of frustration over her inability to manage the classroom, the lack of mentoring, the unwelcoming school culture, and the overwhelmed administrators all contributed to her decision to leave. She was working nights and weekends, was emotionally drained, and anxious. This story saddened me.

The good news at the end of the conversation was that she is still passionate about supporting students. She worked for a nonprofit helping students learn and was running for school board to more widely influence the success of students. We talked about how she was *still a teacher* in her new role and that she was grateful to have found ways to use her gifts and passion to contribute to the profession. As a former teacher her classroom perspective will contribute to the way she leads in her new school board role.

Susan Moore Johnson's research findings are similar to this teacher's story. I first met Susan when I enrolled in her course titled *Teachers at Work* as part of my doctoral studies at Harvard University. She is a former teacher who understands the daily life of schools as well as the big picture of public policy. We shared common interests and often found ourselves at the same conferences advocating for teacher support programs. In her book *Finders and Keepers: Helping New Teachers Survive and Thrive in Our Schools* (2004), she reports the ways in which school culture influences beginning teachers' decisions to stay or leave the profession. Johnson's research shows that inadequate support systems for students, disjointed curriculum, and lack of parent involvement also contributed to new teachers leaving. The pressures of the classroom, the requirements of completing unfamiliar required paperwork, and the documentation for teacher evaluation add to early career teacher stress and anxiety. In her newest book, *Where Teachers' Thrive: Organizing Schools for Success* (2019), she maps out specific ways leaders can build a school community that retains our newest teachers and supports our experienced teachers.

I believe we can positively contribute to teacher retention by systematically supporting our beginning teachers through mentoring and social-emotional support. Healthy role models and mentors among us are needed to give these novices permission to take a break! I wonder how district leaders rationalize spending resources to attract the best and the brightest candidates for their schools, and then scrimp on mentoring and induction programs that support these most vulnerable teachers. What I am also learning is that all teachers need strategies to find balance and calm in their teaching days and lives, not just the beginners! We can do this!

The third question is *Why do teachers stay?* I have been most inspired by the responses from Sonia Nieto's teachers as expressed in the research from her book, *What Keeps Teachers Going?* (2003). I met Sonia in line at the State House where we gathered to protest the elimination of funding from the education budget in the late 1980s. Sonia was a teacher education professor at a public university, and I was a classroom teacher. I fell in love with her work because she wasn't afraid to talk about the real issues facing teachers. One reason that stood out clearly in her research is that most teachers stayed because of their relationships with their students. These teachers talked about their challenges and disappointments, but they also reported their love of teaching. They expressed their faith in public education and this hope kept them going when they struggled with the many disparities they faced in their schools.

These three questions and these authors' perspectives have provided me with the rationale and courage to write this book. It not only takes courage to teach, but it also takes wisdom, balance, and inspiration to stay in teaching.

TEACHER WELL-BEING RELATES TO STUDENT SUCCESS

What will make the biggest difference in improving schools will be bolstering the skills and morale of those who are already on the job.
—Gene Maeroff

I believe raising the morale of teachers will sustain our profession and bring us to new heights of creativity, hope, and optimism. The connections between morale, physical health, social-emotional well-being, and joy of teaching influence teacher retention and the ways in which teachers talk about their work. Most research on social-emotional learning has been focused on how teachers can educate their students to be more mindful in the classroom. Less research has been focused on the social and emotional skills of the teachers and how their well-being can enhance student success in the classroom.

I teach an online course titled *Social-Emotional Learning: Self-Care for All Educators*. It was designed in response to the many teachers in my courses who talked about stress being the biggest challenge for beginning teachers. Mentors heard their beginners saying things like, "The hours are long, the pay is poor, and the paperwork piles up quickly; it's easy to lose sight of why I became a teacher in the first place" (Roberts & Kim, 2019). In the *Harvard Ed. Magazine*, an article titled *PD Also Means Personal Development* (Hough, 2020), Tyler Hester, shares his vision for supporting novice teachers at the beginning of the school year. His program responds to the retention research and fills the gap for early career teachers with social-emotional skills, mindfulness, meditation, and some effective prioritizing processes. Many of these skills are offered to you in the *Mindful Living Actions* section of this book. We all need personal development not just the beginners.

Teachers who are stressed are less likely to form close relationships with their students, and this can negatively impact their success in school. Roberts and Kim (2019) share their recommendation that creating conditions for teachers to thrive instead of *just survive* is the best way to retain healthy teachers. What we need to remember is that the state of "being well" is more than the absence of stress or illness, it is the ability to *express* joy, happiness, and see the positive side of situations so we can move forward with healthy vibrant actions.

We can't really afford to ignore the negative impacts of teacher stress anymore. The negative consequences of teacher stress and overload have been widely discussed in various research studies. *Teacher Stress and Health*, a report from the Pennsylvania State University Robert Wood Johnson

Foundation, documents higher teacher turnover and lower effectiveness in our schools overall (Greenberg, Brown, & Abenavoli, 2016). We can't just keep recruiting new teachers to take the place of those who leave in the first 5 years. We need to focus on the problems of why teachers are leaving and what we can do to model and create the environment we are all seeking.

Many early career teachers arrive early and stay late thinking that if they work harder and longer it will all get better. In fact, it gets worse because now they are exhausted, unbalanced, and can't think clearly about what to do next. Adding this work stress to their personal life creates an overwhelmed feeling, which leads to burnout and often causes beginners to quit. You've heard the stories.

What surprises most teachers in my self-care course is that there are competencies for educator social and emotional learning (Jones, Bouffard, & Weissbourd, 2013). We spend most of our professional learning time focusing on how to teach our students and how to manage their social and emotional skills that we forget that we need to learn these skills, too. The authors state that "[s]tudents learn from the way teachers manage frustration, maintain control of themselves and the classroom, stay focused in the face of distractions, and shift tactics when needed." Embedding social and emotional strategies into a teachers' daily work indicates teachers can be healthy role models for their students and feel better at the same time!

Robert Kegan's research on adult development and his focus in his book *Immunity to Change* (Kegan & Lahey, 2009) help us understand why we react the way we do and also why we sometimes don't react at all! Reflecting on our strengths and unlocking our potential is a first step to taking action.

"But reflection without action is ultimately as unproductive as action without reflection."
—Robert Kegan

I used the inspiration I gained in Kegan's courses to support teacher development at my school, in the district, and in my own course development. I believe what he was saying and understand how it influences teacher development. Kegan's *Minds at Work* initiative takes his academic theories and applies them in the context of real work.

If we truly want to transform the professional culture in our schools, we need to reflect on what we are learning to better understand how to take care of ourselves, support the teachers around us, and learn the social-emotional skills that will help us be healthy and fulfilled. Then we can most effectively help our students succeed.

THE PATH WE CHOOSE

The first poem I ever memorized in junior high school was *The Road Not Taken* by Robert Frost (1916). I refer to it from time to time when I need to be reminded that I have the freedom to choose my path. The last stanza states,

> *I shall be telling this with a sigh,*
> *Somewhere ages and ages hence:*
> *Two roads diverged in a wood,*
> *and I -*
> *I took the one less traveled by,*
> *And that has made all the difference.*

I now see that my ability to listen to myself, to be inspired by the words of others, and to be open to guidance from the world around me has shaped who I am today. By seeing the silver linings in life's disappointments, I am offered another way to look at the circumstances of my ordinary life. The Ten Lessons not only helped balance my emotions, but they also provided me with feelings of renewal, hope, and joy. I now understand them to be my personal mindfulness practices.

WHAT IS YOUR CAREER INTENTION?

Choosing teaching as a career requires a personal sense of purpose and devotion to others. When I was directing the student teacher program at a city university, I was encouraged to participate in a university-wide staff development seminar. It was offered throughout the year, and because it was designed for discussion, only 20 staff members could participate at a time. A Jesuit priest led the sessions and I clearly remember the group was intentionally designed to include a variety of roles from across the campus. The head football coach, a custodian, a teacher educator, a few faculty members from different departments, cafeteria workers, and other members of the college community sat around a large table for several seminar sessions. We learned about each other's roles on campus and how we interacted with the students.

The purpose of the seminar was to understand how our conversations with our students could influence their choice of vocation. The organizers of this seminar understood that many students enter university as undeclared majors. Because students talk to so many people in their school experience, we may all become vocational counselors at some point. The intention behind the seminar was to offer us a way to frame these discussions to be useful to a student's inquiry.

This *vocational discernment* process was created by theology professor Father Michael Himes and introduced us to a questioning process he developed. The seminar encouraged us to shift our conversations from asking our students the typical questions of *What would you like to do or be?* to asking Hime's three questions: (1) What gives you joy? (2) Are you good at it? (3) Does anyone need you to do it?

I was inspired by the process and how it worked with the teacher education students and others members of my family, including my children. I continue to use a modified version of the questions today any time someone asks me for advice about their path. I ask you now, as you hold this book in your hand, *what is your intention*? Do you always plan to stay in the classroom? Does it still give you joy? Are you good at it? Does the profession still need you? Are you drawn to other leadership roles? You may not know the answers to these questions now, and your intention may unfold as you read the Ten Lessons.

Responding to questions and making decisions can cause anxiety, especially if we think we have to make the *right* decision to get to our intended goal. As you think about your intention and read my stories, it may relieve you to know that you don't have to make big decisions to have big shifts in your life. Instead, we need to become more aware of our small daily choices that lead us to our next step. These daily decisions are the mindful awareness steps that ensure we are tapping into what we love to do. Staying awake to these choices and actually seeing them is part of the process. That is how an inspired career in teaching is nurtured and sustained. And the good news is you don't have to make any decisions right now!

In these pages, you'll learn ways you can take small steps to continue your professional growth. One next step may be reading a new book or collaborating with other teachers on implementing an innovative idea. You could even decide to step into a teacher leadership role to support a new program that is evolving. Trust the process. It doesn't have to be perfect. It is just the next step. Each step will have ups and downs. You may not see the connection between this next step and where you'll end up. That is okay. Follow the bread crumbs.

The Road Not Taken poem reminds me that I make a choice each time an option shows up for me and I often choose to take the path less traveled by. The Ten Lessons in this book serve as guiding lights illuminating the path at every turn. Use them to keep you focused on your intention, the one in front of you right now. When I look back at my choices I see that taking the path less traveled by has made all the difference.

WHO HELPS YOU REACH YOUR FULL POTENTIAL?

Many years ago at a professional workshop, I learned how important it is to build

a community of support. The workshop leader introduced a concept called a Circle of Mentors, and she encouraged us to list people who support us in our lives and work. I embraced the idea and envisioned people actually sitting around my kitchen table because that is where all the important decisions were made in my family. This reminded me that I am only as good as the support team around me.

My first Circle of Mentors drawing included the names of the people I turned to when I needed financial advice or emotional support. I even included some of my deceased ancestors who had served as mentors to me throughout my life. I use this process from time to time and have recommended it to both beginning teachers and mentors so they can identify the people in their lives who support them. The process shifts my attitude from one of fear and uncertainty to confidence and clarity. Because I had this trusted circle of mentors around me I could take risks, but I never felt afraid of these next steps.

When I left the classroom I was teaching across the street from where I lived with a 2-minute commute! I chose to drive to a city university more than an hour away. People thought I was crazy! I thought I might be crazy on some days when I sat in traffic for hours. Yet I felt that was where I needed to be. Sure, it was a lot harder to drive there, and learn to be a director, and lead a program that I had to learn first. But it felt right. I was supposed to be doing this work, and I loved it. I draw my circle of support every few years because the circle keeps changing with new people coming into my life. I encourage you to acknowledge who is mentoring you.

WE ARE THE ONES . . .

As teachers we put all our energy into our students, and clearly that is important, but I believe we are at a crucial point when we must focus on ourselves. We have all heard the airline message, "Put your own oxygen mask on first." The rationale for this statement is that we need enough air to breathe and enough energy to move before we can assist or give help to others. Following that line of reasoning, we as teachers should be prioritizing our health and well-being so we can bring our best selves to our classrooms and schools.

This book offers us ways we can keep our oxygen flowing, ways we can keep ourselves as the priority before we look to our students' needs. I thought yoga training would be about mastering the poses or sitting for long periods of time without moving. It wasn't about that at all. I learned the key to any of my practices is about my breath. This book provides us with some time to listen to our breath and be grateful for the life it gives us.

Right now in American education many teachers are feeling the anxiety of designing new curricula and they are questioning how their personal relationships with students can be replicated in new ways. Our relationships with our students, our colleagues, parents, and administrators will probably look different in these new online and hybrid formats. How *we* feel and how we make others feel will influence our teaching—no matter the format we use. By taking care of our needs we will be more aware of the needs of others. How we consciously show up at meetings and in these new learning formats will influence how we make others feel.

Paying attention to how we feel is what this book is about. Can we include teachers' social and emotional well-being as part of this new paradigm for education? This is not the time to be silent or to blame others. It is a time for questions, creative ideas, and listening. One of the teachers in my self-care course created a workshop for teachers at her school. Her motto was, *Happy, healthy teachers make happy, healthy students!* It always makes me smile when I say that phrase. So simple, yet so true!

I first heard these words, "We are the ones we are waiting for," as part of a song titled *We Are the Ones*, sung by Sweet Honey in the Rock (1998). The stage lighting was dimmed, and the song blared from the large speakers in the conference auditorium. I was one of thousands of teachers sitting in a giant room feeling the rhythm of the music. I had chills. The message was clear. WE can be the change we are looking for in our schools. The vibration in the room elevated to one of hope and optimism. The song also left me with a feeling of ownership and responsibility. WE are the seeds of change.

It is easy to become disheartened or frustrated by the decisions and policies made in any school system. It is easy to blame leadership. What many of us forget is that we have the power to expand our sphere of influence beyond the four walls of our individual classrooms to be part of the positive change we seek.

"The most common way people give up power is by thinking they don't have any."
—Alice Walker

When teachers intentionally collaborate to break down silos and stereotypes we can make a difference for our students. If we really want to be part of the changes we think should happen, we have to *believe* we have the power to influence the system. We have to let our inspiration ignite the spark that creates ideas and innovations that will influence change in ourselves and the organizations in which we work. Paying attention to our own health and well-being is a first step to being that change.

So I guess you could say that my career has taken many turns and this is an example of what happens when you *follow the bread crumbs* and they lead you to a next step. I did not map this journey out. In some ways it came to me. If anyone ever said to me in those beginning years of teaching that I would be leading my own company and writing a book about my teaching story, I would never have believed it! Yet here I am. As you read my stories you will understand parts of my journey and how each of these experiences had its challenges and silver linings. The stories seemed overwhelming and insurmountable at the time, and yet when I read them now they are all part of a tapestry: the small steps and choices woven together to create my very big abundant life.

We are the ones we have been waiting for.
—June Jordan

Let's collectively build the educational community we all envision. This is your book, your path, and your career to create as you intend.

Ten Lessons

1

Follow
Your Heart

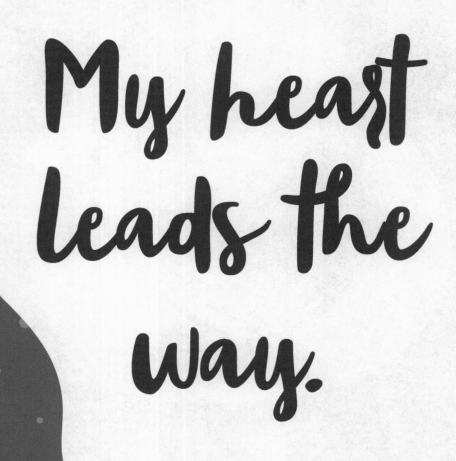

My heart leads the way.

Choosing to Teach

 Podcast Introduction to the Chapter

Do you remember when you decided to become a teacher? Did you always want to teach or did the idea come to you later in life? Did people encourage you or discourage you? There are so many different reasons people choose this career. If you are already teaching you know how well you were prepared for the classroom realities. We all have the same classroom responsibilities, whether you completed a traditional undergraduate program, like I did, or you are a career changer who completed an accelerated program later in life. Finding your wisdom has to begin with why you chose to teach in the first place. That is the beginning of your story. Whether you are a pre-service teacher just deciding now to become a teacher, you are an experienced teacher in the middle of your career, or maybe you are nearing retirement, this is the time to reflect on why you chose to teach. If you find yourself in a role that is not fulfilling, is there another role for you within the education community? There are no right or wrong answers in the business of the heart. Stay open. Listen.

In this chapter you will have an opportunity to reflect on your journey into teaching and revisit your career intention. Use the *Mindful Living Actions* to reveal the joy in your life and work. Celebrate being a teacher.

Wisdom Through Stories

My Story—When the Guidance Counselor Told Me No

Audio Reading by the Author

I have always wanted to be a teacher. My first memories of play include directing my invisible students in my pretend classroom. Some people say it is because I am the oldest child in a family of five and the psychology of birth order aligns with being directive and bossy. My younger siblings would agree. I loved talking about school and envisioned myself teaching "my students" in my own classroom. Because I had selected my path at such an early age, I didn't think about alternate careers or what I would do after high school. I knew I would attend the local teachers' college and become a teacher and everyone around me knew it, too. Everyone except my high school guidance counselor.

Mrs. P. met with me in her tiny crowded office on that fateful day and said, "You won't be able to apply to the teachers' college because your SAT scores are too low." Stunned, I sat there with an uncertain response, not sure of what I was hearing. My effort was outstanding; I was on the honor roll and a member of the prestigious National Honor society. In my opinion my test scores didn't reflect my intelligence or creativity. Mrs. P. explained there was a "cut score" for submitting an application to the teacher program and my scores did not make the cut. I was frustrated, embarrassed, and at a loss for words. My heart sank. I had to be a teacher!

I cringe when I reflect on this story and think about how my life would have turned out differently had I listened to Mrs. P.'s advice.

Three things I did that you may consider doing if you find yourself at a crossroad:

- FIND A MENTOR—I shared my disappointment with my mother. I also shared the embarrassment of my less-than-perfect scores and the sting of hearing no to my dream. She emphatically said, "You are going to college to be a teacher because that is what you were born to do!"

- TRY AGAIN—I registered to retake the SAT, and I studied with a friend who had done well. The scores were a bit higher, but I still didn't make the cut score stated in the application that my counselor suggested.

- DO IT ANYWAY—Then, with my mother's encouragement, I applied to the teaching program with the scores from the retake. I put all my passion into my essay and shared my dream of becoming a teacher from my heart.

I was accepted and successfully completed the program and became a fifth-grade teacher, where I happily taught for more than 20 years. I loved my classroom, my students, and the feeling of following my heart's passion. I went on to complete my master's degree as well as a doctorate at the Harvard Graduate School of Education. My dream came true, and I am still living it.

Hearing no from Mrs. P. was a pivotal point in my life where I could have chosen differently. I learned that another person's advice doesn't have to deter me from following my own heart. I also learned that I could pick myself up after a devastating conversation with my counselor and get some help to achieve a goal. My mother, my advocate and mentor, encouraged me to take the right actions I needed to become a teacher.

I will always consider myself a teacher. When I lose my way and am uncertain about what to do next, I whisper to myself, *"Follow your heart,"* and I know I will find my way to my next teaching opportunity.

Another Teacher's Story

Meet Kathleen Pimental and listen to her story, *My Unexpected Journey Into Teaching.*

Finding Your Wisdom: What's Your Story?

Reflect and respond to the following prompts:

1. How does my story of following my heart relate to you?
2. Why did you choose to become a teacher?
3. How did other people influence your decision to become a teacher?
4. How do you talk to aspiring teachers about choosing to teach?
5. What is your heart telling you at this point in your teaching journey?

FOCUS ON JOY

The word joy brings a smile to my face. It feels warm and happy. When we follow our hearts there is a sense of joy inside us and around us. Who wouldn't want a little joy in their life? Yet it eludes us because we are often distracted by other daily issues that keep our minds busy. Joy relates to the heart. Mindful Living Actions are about intentionally bringing experiences into our lives that move us emotionally. You know when you are in the zone and you find that sweet spot. Words don't capture that vibration of energy when we know we are doing what we are supposed to be doing. For me teaching is that sweet spot. It was my chosen career and it was not an option. It is what I am supposed to be doing. There are many ways to teach though, and the heart will lead the way if you ask the right questions.

ASSESS YOUR TEACHING CAREER

Rate yourself from 1 to 3 (1 disagree – 2 sometimes – 3 agree)

1. I was born to be a teacher.

    ① ② ③

2. My teaching goals include instructional leadership supporting teachers.

    ① ② ③

3. I see myself in administration or public policy to support teachers.

    ① ② ③

4. Teaching is just one of many careers I am exploring.

    ① ② ③

5. Teacher leadership is a way I can contribute while still in my classroom.

    ① ② ③

What is the message you see in your responses?

PRACTICE SELF-CARE

CELEBRATE!—When we achieve an important milestone we often celebrate. Birthdays, anniversaries, and weddings come to mind as joyful celebrations of events in our lives that are meaningful and *full of meaning* to us. These rituals are usually planned in advance and often are *over-the-top* experiences costing so much money that we lose the fun in participating in the event. How many times have we heard someone complaining about wedding plans or *big birthdays* that required perfect coordination so much so that the event itself—the celebration—gets lost in the details? What if we looked at a celebration as a way to actually intentionally bring joy into our day?

TRY THIS!—Choose something you would like to celebrate in your life. This will not be a public event or party, but rather a quiet acknowledgment of something in your life. It may be as simple as waking up and celebrating the new day! Create a ritual to honor this moment. Feel the joy in your heart as you acknowledge this event. A ritual I have done to acknowledge my blessings is to create a nature design. I take a walk in the neighborhood or in a park and collect items from nature. I choose a place to lay my items and with some gratitude and intention I give thanks.

EXPLORE MINDFUL RESOURCES

Learn more about these authors at Resources .Corwin.Com/TeachingWithLight.

Two resources that lift my spirits are *Monday Hearts for Madeline* created by Page Hodel (2009) and *Morning Altars* by Day Schildkret (2018). I love using natural objects to create colorful art, and these books will inspire you to try it.

REMEMBER What Will Support You

- Listen to what your heart is whispering and check in to see if that is where you need to go next. Sit quietly to make sure it is your voice.

- Take action steps to move you in the right direction.

- Seek out a mentor who will encourage you and support you in making the right choice.

- Take a risk! Even if the advice from outside is that you might not be accepted, you can still try or apply!

- See the positive! Look for the silver linings and celebrate your successes. Let go of the past failures or disappointments.

Be Inspired by the Words of Others

LISTEN to Inspiring Leaders

LEARN About Influential Authors and Books

 Meet Jaclyn Roster and listen to how she followed her heart.

Following your heart can be difficult to do if you can't hear what your heart is saying. These authors and books helped me sit still long enough to hear my heart's message. Learn more on the companion website at resources.corwin.com/TeachingWithLight.

Roland S. Barth's book *Improving Schools From Within: Teachers, Parents, and Principals Can Make a Difference* (1990) touched my teacher heart. I dog-eared pages, highlighted words, and wrote in the margins. I could see how he honored teacher wisdom. When I first met Roland in person, on my 40th birthday, I was in awe. He invited me to become one of his graduate students. This is where I learned how a master teacher creates a learning environment where adults can share their varied perspectives. Roland's books and articles helped me find my practical *art of teaching* wisdom.

Two author collaborators, **Kirsten Olson** and **Valerie Brown** (2015) offer a unique leadership book that supports the development of school leaders. *The Mindful School Leader: Practices to Transform Your Leadership and School* integrates mindfulness practices with real-life stories of leaders. I met Kirsten in person one day when I reached out to her as a new Corwin author and asked her advice about writing a new book. Her encouragement and faith in me inspired me to stretch myself.

FEEL Inspiration. This quote has been on my desk for many years, and it reminds me that I am doing what I love.

FOLLOW YOUR BLISS.

—JOSEPH CAMPBELL

2

Bloom Where You're Planted

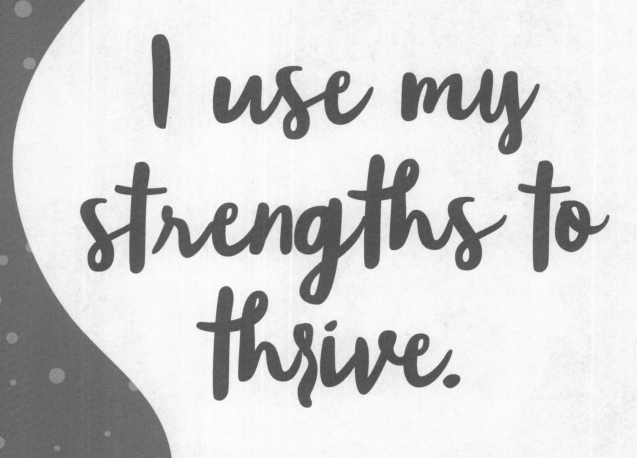

I use my strengths to thrive.

Growing in Place

 Podcast Introduction to the Chapter

Sometimes in our teaching careers it takes courage to stay put, to stay in less than ideal classrooms or schools. Sometimes we need to pause and reflect on what is going on, instead of what we want to be going on. Our mind wants us to escape, run, find a better school, a new grade level, a different administrator, and then everything would be all right. Growth is defined as a process of developing and maturing, a time when we make progress or headway on our goals and purpose. Growing doesn't require us to move anywhere. Maybe we grow more when we stay still?

As I write this message, the country is shut down and we are in the middle of the COVID-19 pandemic. There is nowhere to go. We shelter in place. It is a challenging and tense time for us all, and yet a sense of calm that has emerged from the stillness. I see creativity in teachers who are teaching from home, smiles offered to students and colleagues on virtual platforms. I watch my adult sons cooking elaborate meals, creating home gym routines, and reading books!

There is a sense of peace and beauty growing from the stillness. We are slowing down to a pace where frenzy isn't in charge. Calendars are clear of social events, and there are no sporting events to attend or watch. It is an unusual time in our lives. What is most important to us has become clear.

Natural disasters and crises impact our schools every day: hurricanes, tornadoes, floods, fires, 9/11, and now COVID-19. I believe these challenging and uncertain times are when we see the best in people. Resilience and creativity are brought forth in teachers and students. My story is about my year of teaching in a trailer behind the school and how I grew and matured as a teacher.

In this chapter you will have an opportunity to reflect on the times you saw yourself grow through times of crisis. I believe who we truly are shines through in our darkest hours.

Wisdom Through Stories

My Story—The Year After the School Burned Down

Audio Reading by the Author

My school burned to the ground the year I was accepted into a teaching sabbatical. I became a member of a cohort of teacher leaders released from our teaching duties. Our responsibilities included sharing our successful teaching ideas with schools and university education programs across the state. This was a highlight of my career, and yet at the same time I felt this huge loss beyond words. My classroom was destroyed, and my school was gone. Everything I had created for my elementary classroom was all lost. I had to fulfill my obligation to the fellowship, all the while knowing at the end of the year I had to return to my teaching position, whatever that would be. It was an awkward time for me personally. While teachers from my school were displaced, I was traveling the state sharing ideas in positive settings.

When I returned, I was one of two teachers assigned to teach in one of the portable classrooms parked in the back of the school. My old classroom had colorful learning centers, rugs, special decorations, and personal items for the students. This portable had nothing, except some old desks that hadn't been used in decades. I was devastated. I remember crying on the first day of school as I looked at the trailer. I was going through the grieving process that my colleagues had experienced the year before. Only I was doing it alone.

I felt like a first-year teacher—isolated and overwhelmed. I reached out to my colleague Pat from the fellowship and talked about leaving teaching. I didn't think I could recreate all I had done in my classroom and do it in a trailer! Pat came to visit me. I sobbed. She listened. As she left she handed me a card with the message *Bloom where you're planted* on the front. She encouraged me to stay put and not make a hasty decision to change my teaching assignment, reminding me, "You bring your skills, your years of teaching experience, and your passion for teaching to this moment. Use your strengths."

Based on her advice and my inner resolve I took action in these ways. You may find them useful if you are ever in a crisis.

- ACKNOWLEDGE STRENGTHS—Pat was right. I knew how to teach! I could manage students, modify curriculum, and assess student learning. I loved teaching.

- ASSESS NEEDS—I took an inventory and was able to get new desks, books from the library, and supplies. Since my colleagues had requested materials the year before, I was able to access lots of materials more easily.

- CREATE A LEARNING ENVIRONMENT— I recreated the trailer's boring environment to a magical learning space. With the help of parents and friends, I made this my project. I purchased a director's chair where students could read stories to the class, and we invited guest speakers from the town to talk about their interests.

One of my proudest moments as a teacher happened that year. A student named Billy was waving furiously, trying to get my attention one day near the end of the year. He was shouting, "I finished my book! I did it! I finished the whole book!" Tears came to my eyes as I thought about this student. He was in the fifth grade, and he had been able to hide for all these years that he couldn't read. I noticed this deficit one day. Instead of pointing it out to him or asking him about it, we began to read together every day. And then one day, like magic, he could read on his own.

The crisis of losing my classroom to fire, being placed in a portable trailer in the back of the school, and feeling isolated for a year could have led me to leaving teaching or looking for another position. Instead, it was a year I learned most about who I was as a teacher. I not only bloomed as a teacher, but I was able to help one of my students bloom, too. I learned I really was a good teacher and a teacher can teach anywhere.

Another Teacher's Story

Meet Tammi Penman and listen to her story, *I Don't Want to Move!*

Finding Your Wisdom: What's Your Story?

Reflect and respond to the following prompts:

1. What are your creative gifts and strengths? How do these gifts help you thrive wherever you are?

2. Have you ever had a crisis in your teaching career that you had to overcome? Explain.

3. Share a time in your life when it was better to stay than move on. What was the silver lining to staying put?

4. What is your advice for teachers who are teaching in less than ideal situations?

5. How do students respond and grow when they see their teacher handling tough challenges?

FOCUS ON GROWTH

We grow physically, mentally, emotionally, and spiritually, throughout our lives. We notice children growing in height and maturity, and we see our parents become wiser as they age. What we often do not see is our own growth. We may notice our physical changes, but our internal reflections remain hidden unless we allow them to emerge.

When we take the time to reflect it allows us to recognize our growth as teachers and how we choose to support our development.

Reflection helps us capture the process and look at it for a moment in time. As teachers we are so often in a rush moving to the next activity that we miss the moments of reflection. One day we wake up and notice we have been teaching for so many years it is not worth making a change that would inspire new growth. *Bloom where you're planted* doesn't mean we never move from where we are, however it might mean we choose to stay for a bit and make a conscious choice for our next growth spurt.

ASSESS YOUR TEACHING AND LEADERSHIP SKILLS

Rate yourself from 1 to 3 (1 disagree – 2 sometimes – 3 agree)

1. I bring skills, passion, and knowledge to my teaching.

   ① ② ⓷

2. My leadership skills are developing.

   ① ⓶ ③

3. Teaching is an opportunity for me to share what I know.

   ① ⓶ ③

4. I see that I can contribute to education outside of my classroom.

   ① ② ⓷

5. I am a teacher leader.

   ① ② ⓷

What is the message you see in your responses?

PRACTICE SELF-CARE

READ—How would you like to grow this year? As you reflect on your skills and your leadership desires, think about what you would like to learn. Do you want to learn more about teacher leadership? Do you want to learn how to reflect more systematically to improve your classroom practice?

TRY THIS!—Ask someone you admire in your school or district to recommend an author, a book, or an article that would support your learning and growth. Then read it! Highlight the ideas that stand out to you as important. How can this learning support your development as a teacher? A leader of teachers? What surprised you about this topic?

After your exploration, reflect on your own growth so far as a teacher. Where would you like to grow? How does this new learning influence your choices and direction as you continue to grow in new ways? Put your responses into a visual format.

EXPLORE MINDFUL RESOURCES

Links to these authors' websites are available on the companion website at Resources.Corwin .Com/TeachingWithLight.

Elizabeth Murray's message of *Living Life in Full Bloom* (2014) is that we nurture our lives in tune with the living earth. *Mudras for Modern Life* by Swami Saradananda (2015) offers yoga for your hands and good health.

REMEMBER What Will Support You

- Acknowledge your strengths. Be clear about what you bring to teaching.

- Assess your needs regularly and look outside of yourself for support. You don't have to do everything alone. Ask for help.

- Create spaces for your students, or teachers, to learn. Intentionally focus on what makes a learning environment engaging.

- Reflect on challenges especially during a crisis and understand what it means to stay in the struggle instead of moving away from it.

- *Bloom where you're planted*, especially if it is impossible for you to move!

Be Inspired by the Words of Others

LISTEN to Inspiring Leaders

LEARN About Influential Authors and Books

 Meet Ellyn Metcalf and listen to how she bloomed where she was planted.

Bloom where you're planted tells me to stay put and not to run away from my present circumstances. These authors offered me practical ways to integrate mindful actions into my daily life. Learn more on the companion website at resources.corwin.com/TeachingWithLight.

Jon Kabat-Zinn's book *Wherever You Go There You Are: Mindfulness Meditation in Everyday Life* (1994) gives me practical actions to take to stay in the present moment so I can bloom!

Kabat-Zinn's medical training and integration of mindfulness practices into hospitals demonstrate the power of meditation to reduce pain. His videos, books, and resources offer us all a way in to meditation processes where ever we are.

Kabat-Zinn was a student of **Tích Nhất Hạnh**, and they both believe in the connection of mind, body, and spirit. Tích Nhất Hạnh is a Vietnamese Buddhist monk, peace activist, and founder of the Plum Village Tradition. He has published over 100 books. Three of my favorites are *The Miracle of Mindfulness* (1987); *True Love: A Practice of Awakening the Heart* (1997); and *How to EAT* (2014).

Each of these authors offers us unique ways to integrate mindfulness into our daily lives. It is easy to be mindful and balanced in a meditation class. Doing it in real life is the challenge.

FEEL Inspiration. I met Parker Palmer in a workshop many years ago. I was the one teacher representative sitting among deans, university presidents, and state leaders. He made me feel important.

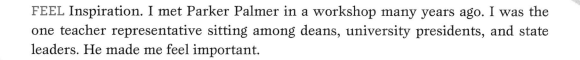

"WE TEACH WHO WE ARE, IN TIMES OF DARKNESS AS WELL AS IN LIGHT."

—PARKER J. PALMER

3

Be a Lamp, Not a Mirror

I shine my light.

Interacting With Adults

 Podcast Introduction to the Chapter

Teacher preparation programs rarely include strategies about how to relate to our colleagues, how to contribute to a school culture in a positive way, or how to be part of a community of adults. Instead, teachers rely on informal guidance such as "Be friendly to the school secretary, buy the custodian coffee and he will help you move your furniture, don't sit in Rachel's seat in the teachers' room," or "The principal doesn't like long faculty meetings so don't ask questions!" Some teachers even say, "It is easier to talk with the students than the adults!"

There are hierarchies in both preK–12 schools and university education departments.

Some of us have worked in both cultures and see the differences and similarities. Both cultures are top-down designs with the administration delivering the directives to the teachers or faculty. Part of the culture of any workplace is based on how freely the teachers can speak and how their suggestions contribute to the decisions made by administration. In places where the teachers' voices are not valued, the teachers' room becomes a hot spot. It can also become a confusing culture for beginning teachers.

We have the freedom to choose who and when to interact with other adults at work. It is not required that we go to the teachers' room. This is the private space where perhaps the most honest sharing of what is going on in a school happens. Some teachers choose isolation in their own classrooms over visiting the teachers' room because they frankly have too much work to do and they don't want to be part of complaining or gossip.

Beginning teachers are unaware of the hidden cultural norms. Some novices have shared that they left teaching because of the disconnect between the complaining in the teachers' room and the lack of open decision making among teachers and administrators.

In this chapter you will have a chance to think about how you interact with other adults and how you can positively influence your work environment. We all have a part to play, and I believe it begins with an open heart.

Wisdom Through Stories

My Story—The Teachers' Room

Audio Reading by the Author

My friend Carol and I used to walk each morning before we went to work. I was a beginning teacher, and she was a counselor working in a residential treatment program. This was our sacred time to talk and process all that was going on in our lives and at work. It was usually very early in the morning, and in these darkest hours we had our most honest and intimate conversations. We lamented about our kids who wouldn't do their chores, husbands who came home late, and work colleagues who just plain aggravated us. We'd complain, share, blame, and at the end of the walk we would feel so much better. Why? We believed it was because we had a chance to get all that "bad stuff" out of our systems before we began our workday. When we missed one of our walks, I noticed I had more angst during the day and could be more easily caught off balance.

One day I had a particularly difficult conversation with a colleague in the teachers' room, and I wasn't sure how to respond. After sharing the situation, Carol said, "Be a lamp, not a mirror!" I replied, "What the heck does that mean?" I didn't really feel like being nice to someone who was being mean to me. Carol's rationale, from her counselor perspective, was that instead of mirroring back the

negative vibes from that teacher, I should shine my light and express positivity.

As a beginning teacher I didn't want to stay away from my colleagues and eat in my room alone. Teaching is hard, and I wanted adult contact. I needed social interaction with my teacher colleagues, but I didn't want to get into negative conversations either.

After discussing all this on my morning walks, Carol and I decided how we could be more like "lamps" in our workplaces. Here are three things I did to make a positive impact in the teachers' room. You may want to try some of these in your home or at work.

- BE QUIET—If someone made a negative or critical comment about a student, family, or administrator, I would NOT ADD to the story. I would not repeat the story or share a similar story that piggybacked on this complaint.

- CONTRIBUTE POSITIVELY—I would contribute a positive story as often as possible. This might be a great idea I just found, something a student did well, or just something in my life that was going well.

- STAND UP—If a person was being discussed in a critical way and I did not have that same experience, I didn't argue or try to add to the story. I just said, "That is not my experience of her. She was really helpful to me. I am sorry your experience isn't the same." This helped me break the gossip cycle and show that this might not be true for everyone.

I really wanted to be part of the group and to have others acknowledge me for my hard work as a beginner. I learned that if I mirrored the complaints and negative behavior of the teachers' room just to be accepted as part of the group, it didn't make me feel any better. In fact it made me feel worse!

I also learned that I had my own light inside of me, and I could offer a smile to someone instead of taking their negative emotions and mirroring them back as my own. I believe the teachers' room doesn't have to be a place of complaint and gossip. It can be a place of sharing and collaboration. So when I find myself in a relationship or in a group of naysayers, I whisper to myself, "Be a lamp, not a mirror," and then I smile.

Meet Angela Barnes and listen to her story, *I Didn't Know What I Didn't Know.*

Finding Your Wisdom: What's Your Story?

Reflect and respond to the following prompts:

1. Have you ever heard the saying "Be a lamp, not a mirror" before? What does it mean to you?

2. How does this message of interacting with adults and my story of the teachers' room relate to you?

3. How did school culture affect you when you were a beginning teacher?

4. Share some examples of when you have been a positive influence in shifting culture in your school for adults.

5. How do you intentionally focus on the positive in your life and work?

FOCUS ON YOUR HEART

Having an open heart means you share openly and honestly. Openhearted people can express warm and kind feelings in ways that touch others' hearts. This truthful communication is comforting because we are so often on automatic pilot that we forget to stop and relate to someone from the heart. We have forgotten how it feels when someone talks with us this way. Little babies and small children so often are just in the moment and we can see their hearts and joy just exuding from them. As adults we tend to leave that state of grace when we fill up our days with doing things and being distracted by technology and outside influences. Opening our hearts is an intentional action. When I smile I can feel the warmth from my heart.

Sharing that light with others brings more light and warmth to our work spaces and homes. We don't even have to say anything out loud to get the benefit.

ASSESS YOUR POSITIVE PERSPECTIVE

Rate yourself from 1 to 3 (1 disagree – 2 sometimes – 3 agree)

1. My colleagues and/or family would describe me as a half-full person.

   ① ② ③

2. I see the silver lining in difficult situations.

   ① ② ③

3. Repeating gossip about others is something I avoid.

   ① ② ③

4. When life brings me lemons I make lemonade

   ① ② ③

5. My luck seems to be bad most of the time.

   ① ② ③

What is the message you see in your responses?

PRACTICE SELF-CARE

SHARE—When you open your heart you are able to share your positive perspective in a way that lifts others up. This authentic gesture brings your true nature forward and allows you to see the light in others, too. Think about how you already share with others. What do you bring to the sharing? What do you most enjoy sharing: a meal, a movie, a conversation?

TRY THIS!—Before you can share your light you need to see it first. Look at yourself in the mirror. Do you see what is beautiful about you, or do you focus on your perceived flaws? Can you see a sparkle in your eyes? Our light is transmitted through our bodies. The way we hold ourselves and the way we intentionally see our light matters. What is shining from within you? Why are you hiding it? I remember the first time I did this process. It was part of a healthy living workshop I was attending. It was called the *mirror process*, and we had to do it every day. I must admit it was very difficult for me. Slowly I got more comfortable and was able to see my good points and my smile.

EXPLORE MINDFUL RESOURCES

The link to these authors' websites are available on the companion website at Resources.Corwin.Com/TeachingWithLight.

DailyOM: Inspirational Thoughts for a Happy, Healthy, and Fulfilling Day by Madisyn Taylor (2008) offers us short inspiring passages that relate to real life. *The Self-Care Prescription* by Robyn L. Gobin (2019) also provides powerful solutions to manage stress and increase well-being.

REMEMBER What Will Support You

- See the positive in your classrooms and schools and share it with your colleagues to make it more visible.

- Speak up when you hear something being said about a colleague or administrator that is not aligned with your experience of that person.

- Be quiet. Sometimes what you don't say is more powerful than what you do say. Not adding to a negative conversation is powerful.

- Encourage complainers to bring an issue to the person who can do something about it instead of just talking about it.

- Smile! You can influence the energy in a room through your positive actions and reactions.

Be Inspired by the Words of Others

LISTEN to Inspiring Leaders

LEARN About Influential Authors and Books

Meet April Frazier and listen as she shares how to be a lamp instead of a mirror.

Be a lamp, not a mirror is a deep, inspirational message for me. Reading these books supported me in looking at the darkness as well as the light. More information is available on the companion website at resources.corwin.com/TeachingWithLight.

My first introduction to **Parker Palmer**'s work was reading *Let Your Life Speak: Listening to the Voice of Vocation* (2000). This small book is packed with stories that reveal Palmer's inner dark thoughts when he could not find his light. It helped me tell the truth about my own feelings and the teaching path I found myself on. Reading *The Courage to Teach: Exploring the Inner Landscape of a Teacher's Life* (Palmer, 1998) helped me acknowledge my personal power as a teacher. I had the opportunity to participate in a weekend retreat with Parker where I learned about the Center for Courage and Renewal.

Sam Intrator, a colleague and friend of Parker's, edited a collection of teachers' stories. This authentic collection, *Stories of the Courage to Teach: Honoring the Teacher's Heart* (2002) inspired me to pay attention to my stories, too. Our stories bring our light out for others to see. He also coedited two amazing poetry books with Megan Scribner that I have used in many of my courses and workshops. *Teaching With Heart* (2014) and *Teaching With Fire* (2003) offer us tender stories and inspiring poetry suggested by teachers. These books help us not only find our light, but also shine it brightly.

FEEL Inspiration. I learned about Yogi Bhajan's life and his teachings in my yoga teacher training program. I share this quote in my workshops to remind us all to recognize and share our light.

TRAVEL LIGHT, LIVE LIGHT, SHARE THE LIGHT, BE THE LIGHT.

—YOGI BHAJAN

4

Face the Sun and the Shadows Will Fall Behind You

I focus on the positive.

Leave Your Troubles at the Door

 Podcast Introduction to the Chapter

Somewhere at the beginning of my teaching career someone told me that I should never bring my personal problems into the classroom. I can't remember who it was or when it was, but it has stayed with me my entire career. The message I held on to was that the students didn't need to know my business. They were in class to learn, and if I came to the classroom upset or teary-eyed, I would upset them and make them uncomfortable.

The messenger also highlighted that the students were not my friends. I was the teacher, and they were in the classroom to learn. I do remember this message didn't mean I should be stern or not share personal information about myself, it was really just about bringing my troubles into the classroom.

I took this message to heart, and it worked well for me because when I did have upsets from home or in my family, I would leave them at the school door and take a respite from these emotional issues. I believe the ways in which we separate our personal emotions and crises is a skill that can be mastered. When we turn our attention away from the dark cloud and toward an activity that keeps us busy we give our mind something to do! The mind is always looking for action and problem solving. So this skill was really important to me when a "perfect storm" of crises entered my life. Looking back on that year, I see my resilience in action, and now I can acknowledge the strength it took for me to teach and focus on the students in my classroom. We can learn how to minimize our black clouds and focus on the positive events in our lives if we intentionally take actions that support our well-being.

In this chapter you will have an opportunity to reveal your inner resilience and acknowledge the times you have "faced the sun" when your life may have been at a low point.

Wisdom Through Stories

My Story—Teaching Through Divorce, Death, and Dissertation

Audio Reading by the Author

We all have struggles in our lives. Ups and downs are part of being human. In my middle 40s I was struggling with my identity and individuality, classic midlife crisis some would say. The internal emotional conversations I was having needed the guidance of a trained professional, so like many people I found a therapist to help me sort out those feelings. I found it comforting and validating to have someone listen to my thoughts, but also frustrating to not get any answers.

Three years earlier I had changed my teaching focus from the fifth-grade classroom to lead a student teaching program at a university more than an hour away. The long commute, the new role as a director of student teaching, and a new identity as a program leader contributed to my unsettled feelings. In addition to all these professional challenges, my relationship with my husband was strained.

After much deep reflection I decided to separate from my husband of 24 years. When I told my parents, I will never forget my father asking me, "Are you happy?" Admitting that I was not happy brought up feelings of failure and shame. I felt torn and emotionally insecure. I had two sons who needed my love and care. My inner voice and soul felt the honesty of my decision, even though it would take great courage to proceed.

Soon after my decision to leave my marriage, my father's lung cancer recurred. Commuting to work, visiting the hospital almost daily, and finalizing a divorce were all happening at the same time. To add to the emotional chaos, I was in the final stages of completing and submitting my doctoral dissertation. I was depleted, unfocused, and confused. When I mistakenly deleted the final chapter of my dissertation, I lost my will to complete the task. At that moment, I dropped to my knees and sobbed. This was the last straw. I second-guessed all my decisions and spent the day in emotional turmoil and tears over the lost work and the confusing challenges I was facing in my life.

A friend sent me a card with the phrase "Face the sun and the shadows will fall behind you" printed on the front. I repeated the words several times and felt a shift in my energy. The words touched my heart. I said to myself, "Look at the positive, Carol. Find your light." Then I heard a tiny voice inside of me say, "Don't quit now. Your father would not want you to quit." So I intentionally shifted my thoughts and energy. I moved toward the light by taking action. I rewrote the final chapter and submitted it on time.

Three things I did that you may consider doing if you find yourself in desperate times.

- FIND MOTIVATION—I dedicated my dissertation to my dad. That action of typing the dedication page motivated me to complete the final chapter.

- GET HELP—I stayed in counseling. I went weekly to process my emotions in a healthy way so I could see the good that still existed in my life.

- GO TO SCHOOL—I went to school every day and left my troubles at the door. It was a relief to have a break each day and not think about my personal issues.

What I love most about this expression is that it gives me an intentional direction to look for the positive, the light, and the good instead of focusing on what is not working. When I look back at this phase of my life I see the enormous pain and suffering, but I also see my strength and my willingness to shift.

Another Teacher's Story

Meet Jimmy Knuuttila and listen to his story, *I Choose to Teach Again*.

Finding Your Wisdom: What's Your Story?

Reflect and respond to the following prompts:

1. Is there such a thing as work-life balance? How do you balance?
2. When have you needed help in your life? How did you *Face the Sun*?
3. How does your personal life influence your teaching?
4. How does the message "leave your troubles at the door" relate to you?
5. What do you do to stay positive and get yourself out of despair?

Mindful Living Actions

FOCUS ON GRATITUDE

When we are suffering and our lives are filled with pain it is difficult to find that place where we can be grateful. Sometimes our lives and work can just be overwhelming. *Facing the sun* means to see the beauty and to see the positive in the situation.

For me healing my personal hurts helps open up the space for gratitude to come in. Healing is a process of becoming healthy again. It allows us to relieve and lesson our suffering. The first step toward healing is to shift our perspective away from what has caused the pain and look instead at what is beautiful around us. Then gratitude can emerge to give us voice to what we indeed are grateful for in our lives.

ASSESS YOUR SOCIAL AND EMOTIONAL SKILLS

Rate yourself from 1 to 3 (1 never think about it – 2 sometimes pay attention – 3 very mindful)

1. I recognize my emotions and how they influence my behavior.

   ① ② ③

2. My perspective includes empathy for others.

   ① ② ③

3. I manage my emotions in a healthy way to minimize stress.

   ① ② ③

4. I am motivated to create personal and professional goals.

   ① ② ③

5. My choices are based on how they impact my health and well-being.

   ① ② ③

What is the message you see in your responses?

PRACTICE SELF-CARE

LISTEN—Before we can be grateful, we need to be able to diminish our hurts and pains. Sometimes we don't even know what is hurting us emotionally; we just feel hurt. One way to reveal what is bothering us is to write in a dialogue journal. This allows us to write some questions and then respond to them intuitively. We spend a lot of time talking to others about what isn't working, complaining about problems we face, and processing relationships. All that talking from outside ourselves can bring mixed messages and lots of confusion. When we stop and become still, we can hear our inner voice. Listening encompasses more than our ears. We listen with our entire body.

TRY THIS!—Dedicate some time to listen to your inner voice. Ask yourself what you need to know right now about your past hurts so you can move forward to find gratitude. Write your reflections by hand with paper and pen. Be patient and let the words flow from your pen. Design a "gratitude box" and keep it near your bed along with small slips of paper and a pen. Add one thing to your box each day before you go to bed. At the end of the month, read all you are grateful for and notice how this makes you feel.

EXPLORE MINDFUL RESOURCES

The link to this book and more about the 7 Mindsets is available on the companion website at resources.corwin.com/TeachingWithLight.

Ridiculously Amazing Schools: Creating a Culture Where Everyone Thrives (2019) came to me by accident. A former student teacher introduced me to Tracey Smith and coauthor Jeff Waller. I was so inspired by this book I read it in one day!

REMEMBER What Will Support You

- Take action to motivate yourself to shift your perspective. I dedicated my dissertation to my dad. What would work for you?

- Seek out professional help if you are struggling—no blame, no shame. This personal time to listen to what makes your soul happy will guide you.

- Go to school and leave your troubles at the door. Students and colleagues don't need to process your woes.

- Find healthy ways to balance your home life and your school life. Balance is key when you are juggling many responsibilities.

- Listen to your inner wisdom, and use it to guide you as you make decisions that impact your personal and professional life.

Be Inspired by the Words of Others

LISTEN to Inspiring Leaders

LEARN About Influential Authors and Books

 Meet Tracey Smith and listen to the ways she helps teachers face the sun.

Face the sun and the shadows will fall behind you is a message of hope and renewal. These authors and their artist processes influenced the way I looked at my memories. They helped me release what no longer served me so I could move forward. To learn more about these authors, visit the companion website at resources.corwin.com/TeachingWithLight.

Michael Samuels and Mary Rockwood Lane's (2013) book *Healing With The Arts: A 12 Week Program to Heal Yourself and Your Community* was recommended to me by a close friend. The experience of expressing myself through various art forms and reflecting on my life's purpose gave me great comfort and peace. Mary's story of emerging from a dark depression offers hope. Her free course is on her website.

Julia Cameron's (2016) *The Artist's Way: A Spiritual Path to Higher Creativity* helped me personally process some of my own dark times. The process of daily journaling and artist dates is one I return to when I need to focus on what is most meaningful to me. I like the hard copy book and journal, but the online version offers options to select the chapters that are most meaningful to you. To *find the sun and face into its light* means we need to find the tools that will support us in moving away from the darkness. These books supported me on my teaching path.

FEEL Inspiration. I discovered Dyer's book, *Change your thoughts, change your life* (2009), and it influenced the way I looked at my relationships and the events occurring around me.

WHEN YOU CHANGE THE WAY YOU LOOK AT THINGS, THE THINGS YOU LOOK AT CHANGE.

—WAYNE DYER

5

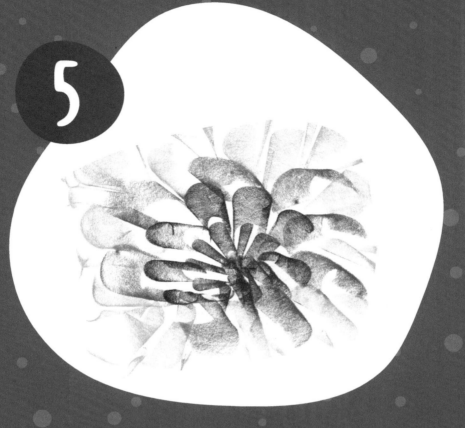

Be a Ripple

My positive
energy
supports
others.

Creating a Collaborative Community of Teachers

 Podcast Introduction to the Chapter

Curriculum originates from state leaders, district central offices, school boards, and committees, but it is the teachers who have to implement the ideas in the classroom. Teachers bring the magic to teaching. They not only have to engage an audience and convince them that this topic is worth learning, but they also have to understand the underlying principles of the content and assess the success of delivering this information to the students. A tall order for any profession! And how do teachers do this day in and day out? We learn by doing it. We learn what works and what we should never do again. There is little time for sharing the success stories with other teachers or paying attention to our own education-related learning topics.

Teacher sharing is either nurtured or minimized. The principal has a major role in how sharing ideas among teachers is embraced. A school leader who encourages teachers to *come out of the classroom* and share their ideas validates their expertise and demonstrates an understanding that schools thrive when teachers collaborate. If the district fosters a competitive environment, teachers tend to keep their good ideas close and there is little room for sharing. Are teachers at your schools competing for high test scores, or are they sharing ideas so all teachers in the school achieve success?

A collaborative environment encourages individual teachers to rise and shine in their areas of expertise, and it also encourages them to share what they learn. I believe a collaborative community of teachers is one way to *share our magic* with our beginning teachers so they don't have to continuously reinvent the wheel to learn how to teach most effectively. It takes energy to share ideas. We have to be motivated from the heart to see our collaboration as contributing to the collective good of the organization. We also must see our goal is to support our students' success in school. Otherwise why would we bother?

In this chapter you will have an opportunity to rediscover what you love to teach and how you can share your successes with others. Teaching the district curriculum is required, but that doesn't mean we stop learning and participating in education topics that bring us joy. When we integrate our love of learning into our teaching, our students notice.

Wisdom Through Stories

My Story—Simply Sharing Is Not So Simple!

Audio Reading by the Author

I submitted a fair number of grant proposals during my career, and most required a list of ways I would share what I learned. One of my first memories of being a ripple was when I designed an interactive workshop for the teachers at my school. The workshop was "Simply Sharing," because I wanted my colleagues to know that it was not a presentation—everyone would simply share an idea for 5 minutes. The flyer read, "Bring one idea to share, there will be refreshments and a door prize!" Music was playing as teachers arrived, and I made sure there were delicious refreshments, including chocolate! At the end of the session someone volunteered to host the next sharing circle. Collaborative sharing was born at our school—an important shift in our school culture started with just a few teachers!

With this successful spark, a small group of us thought it was time to offer a district-wide professional development program. We expanded our core group to include preK–12 teachers and met with the superintendent to propose a new program for teacher-to-teacher sharing. Using the funds that usually went to outside speakers, we would take responsibility for 3 half days during the school year.

Our goal was to feature 12 teachers from the district. The teacher leaders selected had to be passionate and enthusiastic about sharing their idea beyond their own classrooms. Participants from all grade levels could register for any workshop topic. We had all attended the one-and-done type of professional development sessions, so we designed these workshops to meet three times during the year. This follow-up provided time to refine practice in the classroom, leave room for questions, and allow for more interaction with the topic. We even included a book club, a documentary education film discussion, a design your own workshop, and an opportunity for independent study. The next year we added school site visits where teachers could go to another district to learn how they approached a certain topic.

Three things I learned about developing opportunities for sharing ideas that you may want to try.

- MAKE IT PRACTICAL—Any professional development program for teachers needs to be practical and relevant to what is needed in the classroom. The teachers we invited to lead workshops were well respected and passionate about their topics.

- FIND LIKE-MINDED COLLEAGUES—Create a preK–12 team and design roles for others teachers to visibly lead parts of the program so you are not the lone leader.

- GET BUY-IN—Start with activities that align to district and state program goals to ensure administrators support the collaborative norm you are creating. Assess and report the results to all stakeholders.

The successful implementation of this unique professional development model not only broke down some of the stereotypes and judgments we had about teachers from other grade levels, but it also created a unity in the district where we started to get to know and care for other educators in different schools.

Being a ripple is not easy. It must be intentional, practical, and come from a place of passion. Creating a collaborative culture among teachers in schools is a powerful way to improve schools from within. Ripples flow out from a center point. Someone has to throw the first pebble into the pond. Why not you?

Meet Jayla Watje and listen to her story, *Every Teacher is a Teacher of Reading.*

Finding Your Wisdom: What's Your Story? Sharing With Others

Reflect and respond to the following prompts:

1. How does my message about collaboration relate to you?
2. What does "be a ripple" mean to you?
3. How do your *energy levels* influence your work and play?
4. Have you ever stepped up to organize teacher sharing? If yes, explain. If not, why not?
5. What are your skills, passions, and talents that could benefit other teachers?

Mindful Living Actions

FOCUS ON ENERGY

We all need energy to do our work and be motivated to complete the tasks that life presents to us. The more we know about our own energy levels and how we operate the better for us. I like to stay up late and sleep later in the morning. Other friends are early to bed and early to rise. Finding our rhythm is important to how we are able to share and contribute to the greater good. We can't ripple out energy we don't have inside us.

ASSESS YOUR ABILITY TO LEARN AND SHARE

As a teacher you have been in school most of your life either learning curriculum as a student or teaching required curriculum from the district.

When do you learn what you are interested in? How do you collaborate?

Rate yourself from 1–3 (1 disagree – 2 never think about it – 3 agree)

1. I consider myself a lifelong learner.
   ① ② ③

2. I encourage others to learn and share.
   ① ② ③

3. Sharing comes naturally to me, and I participate in groups.
   ① ② ③

4. I have sought out opportunities to share my ideas.
   ① ② ③

5. I model sharing for my students by sharing with other teachers.
   ① ② ③

What is the message you see in your responses?

PRACTICE SELF-CARE

MOVE—Movement requires motivation and energy. Stand up and put your arms up over your head. Yes, that took physical energy and mental commitment to actually do it. Did you actually do it? Commitment to share and ripple out ideas also requires energy and movement. Ripples move out from a central core. Someone has to begin that ripple. Whether you are trying to move physical parts of your body to stretch or exercise or you are trying to move an idea or a program, you can be the source of energy that begins the process.

TRY THIS!—Learn something new that includes physical body movement. Consider dance, qigong, golf, running, tai chi, yoga, or any activity that you would enjoy. I practice qigong using videos from YouTube and love the way my energy feels at the end of a short session with Jeffrey Chand.

EXPLORE MINDFUL RESOURCES

You can find the links to these qigong resources at resources.corwin.com/TeachingWithLight.

I first learned about energy work when I completed a level 1 Spring Forest Qigong class by Master Chunyi Lin. Later, when I visited an acupuncturist for chronic pain and she suggested I practice qigong, I discovered Jeffrey Chand on YouTube, and I use his short routines regularly.

REMEMBER What Will Support You

- Teachers like to learn ways to enhance learning for their students. Create teacher sharing opportunities that are relevant to ensure teacher attendance at the sessions.

- Engage other teachers in the effort to promote formal organized sharing. It is easier to work in a group than be that one lone teacher who has a good idea.

- Get administrative support first. We all know how this works. Getting buy-in is crucial to implementation.

- Acknowledge what you are doing well in the classroom. Ask yourself how you can share your ideas with beginning teachers and your colleagues.

- Seek out resources and grants that could personally support your passions for learning new ideas. And then share them! Be a ripple.

Be Inspired by the Words of Others

LISTEN to Inspiring Leaders

LEARN About Influential Authors and Books

 Meet Kat Johnston and listen to her vision for teacher collaboration and sharing.

Be a ripple means we are not alone on our journey. When we intentionally create ideas and dreams to benefit the common good, we must find ways to share these ideas. One of my friends recommended both of these books to me at different points in my career.

Elizabeth Gilbert's (2015) book *Big Magic: Creative Living Beyond Fear* took me by surprise. This personal story of how she gets her ideas and begins and endures through her writing process gave me an insider's view of a dedicated committed author. How she describes her big ideas and the ways in which they move from potential authors made me smile. She gave me permission to think BIG, to take risks, and to keep sharing my ideas with others.

Rippling requires us to seek out networks and audiences to share with. Conferences, workshops, teacher professional development, books, and courses are all ways we can offer our work. The most powerful shift to sharing ideas for me came when I read the book, *Resonate*, by **Nancy Duarte** (2010). This book is about how to tell a story and use images, art, and short messages to talk to the brain in a different way. I must admit this book blew me away. I never went back to the power point narrative text slides again, and I taught my teacher candidates how to use this presentation format with their students. Having great ideas and then being able to share them clearly is what it takes to ripple effectively.

FEEL Inspiration. *The Tao of Leadership* book was given to me when I was taking my first leadership step. This edition by John Heider (2014) continues to guide me. This excerpt from the passage titled "The Ripple Effect" is one of my favorites.

DO YOU WANT TO BE A POSITIVE INFLUENCE IN THE WORLD? FIRST GET YOUR OWN LIFE IN ORDER. YOUR BEHAVIOR INFLUENCES OTHERS THROUGH A RIPPLE EFFECT. A RIPPLE EFFECT WORKS BECAUSE EVERYONE INFLUENCES EVERYONE ELSE. POWERFUL PEOPLE ARE POWERFUL INFLUENCES.

—LAO TZU

6

It Is What It Is

I Know I Am Right

 Podcast Introduction to the Chapter

I like to be right. I see a situation a certain way, and that is the way I think everyone sees it. Sometimes I can persuade others to see it my way, and other times they believe they are right. This creates a tug of war where we go back and forth with our points of view trying to convince the other person to see it our way. Some people manipulate the other person by smiling and nodding and moving in to get their way at the end of the conversation. I tend to be more direct using facts, explaining why I am right, persuading the listener, and pushing hard to convince them of my perspective.

If I see something that is unfair and I can present a better solution, I will bring it up and present my case. I feel if I make a good case it will influence the outcome. Most of the time it works for me because I am passionate about my position, and the solution is usually welcomed. Other times people see the situation differently, and they are not open to another opinion. Whether this happens at home, in our personal relationships, or at school with our colleagues or administrators, dis-agreements influence our emotional state and ability to participate.

I am learning that I have the freedom to make decisions that serve my highest good. This means that when I hold on to a grudge or bad feelings because I don't get my way, it doesn't serve me. In this chapter I share a story highlighting a time when I felt unfairly treated. In the bigger scheme of things, holding on to being *right* can cost us the harmony and balance we are all seeking. This story is an example of me not being persuasive enough to change a situation that I saw as unfair. That is not the lesson I learned from the experience. The story is about how I learned to let go. I continue to learn this lesson over and over to this day.

In this chapter you will reflect on your own memories of being right and reveal what you do to maintain your balance in times that seem unfair to you.

Wisdom Through Stories

My Story—But It's Not Fair!

Audio Reading
by the Author

Part of teaching in my school included duties unrelated to the classroom. These student supervision duties were assigned by the principal each year. The principal's rationale was these were opportunities for the teachers to interact with the students outside of the classroom and see how they related to their friends. We knew that there were no volunteers or paid aides to do the supervision and that, legally, the students needed to be overseen.

We quickly figured out the best duties and the worst duties. Clearly outside recess with more than 200 students in snowy weather for 30 minutes was deemed the bad one. Cafeteria duty could be horrible, but at least you were inside! The other duties were 10-minute *easy* duties and flew by. If we wanted to work in our classrooms and had a long duty, we would groan. No one liked duties, and we didn't buy the "build a relationship" idea the principal was pitching.

The assignment schedule came to us every year on teacher opening day. I noticed that I had a duty every day and everyone else on the team had a free day. The way the schedule rotated some teachers were never assigned the *worst* duties. After 2 years of the same schedule copied and distributed I decided to speak to the principal. He said he would look into it. Nothing changed. I was upset and returned to the principal who didn't want to make a change now, and he suggested that I talk with my colleagues. Well, you can imagine a beginning teacher asking her colleagues to rotate the duties so it would be fair and everyone would share the longer duties didn't go over well. I was upset, confused by the lack of leadership, and frustrated by the reactions of my colleagues. I remember sharing the upset with a friend and she said, "It is what it is!"

Instead of hearing this expression as a failure to persuade someone to see my point of view, I felt a huge release. I think I actually started laughing. Just saying the phrase out loud gave me that same feeling as dropping the tug-of-war rope. I felt free to let go.

As I reflect on this moment in time, I see that I took three actions that helped me process my feelings. You may want to try them if you find yourself in a situation that seems unfair.

- REFLECT—I asked myself, in the larger scheme of life do I really want to obsess on doing an extra supervision duty? The answer, of courses, was no I do not!

- CHOOSE—I had to consciously choose to not be a victim. I had to let go of being right and let go of the feelings of being treated unfairly.

- MOVE ON—I had to accept that this was the schedule. I made my case, and it was not going to change.

I actually don't remember what happened the next year. I think the schedule did change but it didn't matter to me because I had changed my perspective to focus on what was really more important to me. This memory and story is not about how I failed to convince my colleagues or the principal, it is more about letting go of a position and learning where to put my energy. I share this story not so you will give up when you see something unfair or unjust and just accept it. I share it because we get to choose what we stand up for, and sometimes *it just is what it is*, and that is ok.

Meet Marina Vacanti and listen to her story,
I'll Do What It Takes to Teach.

Finding Your Wisdom: What's Your Story?

Reflect and respond to the following prompts:

1. How does my message about being right relate to you?
2. Do you ever say, "It is what it is"? Explain.
3. How does your *freedom* to choose your attitude influence your actions?
4. When have you felt unfairly treated, and what did you do about it?
5. How do you know when it is time to let go of something and move on?

Mindful
Living
Actions

FOCUS ON FREEDOM

We don't often think about the word *freedom* but it is an important one for us to consider. We have the freedom to make choices in our lives. We are in control of the way we react to situations, create learning environments, and create relationships.

One way we use our freedom relates to how we organize our work space in our homes and at school. A teacher's classroom space is an important issue because we use it to teach as well as to store all our materials. Our work space is filled with books, paper, computers, desks, and supplies. How we choose to organize our work space demonstrates how we approach our work to create a learning environment.

ASSESS YOUR TEACHING AND LEARNING ENVIRONMENTS:

Rate yourself from 1 to 3 (1 disagree – 2 sometimes – 3 agree)

1. My home office and school desk are cluttered and messy.

   ① ② ③

2. I consistently clear and purge all materials that are no longer relevant.

   ① ② ③

3. I teach more effectively when my space is clear and beautiful.

   ① ② ③

4. My computer, desk, and/or files are organized. I can easily retrieve information.

   ① ② ③

5. I am emotionally attached to my resources and save everything, just in case.

   ① ② ③

What is the message you see in your responses?

PRACTICE SELF-CARE

SEE—Take a real hard look at your workspaces at home and at school. What do you actually see? I believe our stuff holds energy and memories. How many times have you picked something up and questioned whether you needed it? Classroom organization and being able to retrieve information is critical for teachers. I have personally spent hours looking for a document that I didn't label correctly or put in the proper file. Looking for materials causes a lot of stress. How does your physical space represent your teaching style and learning environment?

TRY THIS!—Select *one* space at school or at home that you would like to organize and make more usable. It may be the top of your desk, a file cabinet, or that junk drawer. Envision what the cleared, clean space will look like when you are done. Before putting anything back ask yourself, "Does this belong here? Do I love it?" If the answer is no then let it go. *See* the beauty in your workspace. Add some items to your desk that inspire you. How do you feel about your newly organized space?

EXPLORE MINDFUL RESOURCES

Links to these books and the authors' websites are available at resources.corwin.com/Teaching WithLight.

I learned about feng shui years ago and applied the principles in my classroom, office, and home. The decluttering processes in Kingston's book, *Clear Your Clutter With Feng Shui* (1999) and *The Western Guide to Feng Shui* by Terah Kathryn Collins (1999) still guide me today. Nicole Gabai from B.Organized (http://www.b-organized.net/) also helped me make sense of my space and how to prioritize my goals.

REMEMBER What Will Support You

- Reflect on a situation that may feel unfair and see how feelings of being right relate to your emotional state. See the other person's point of view.

- Instead of holding on to a grudge or an upset that you can't do anything about, choose your reaction based on what best supports your well-being.

- Discover when it is time to move on and let go of the emotional attachment to being right. Think about how important this issue is in the bigger picture.

- Accept the things you cannot control. Remember you have the freedom to choose actions that support you.

- Minimize stress by clearing your classroom or home office clutter so you can find materials easily. Let go of your emotional attachment to your stuff and add beauty to your learning environment.

Be Inspired by the Words of Others

LISTEN to Inspiring Leaders

LEARN About Influential Authors and Books

 Meet Jennifer Abrams and listen to her message related to *It Is What It Is.*

Nature always demonstrates for us that *it is what it is.* It surrounds us, and yet we often miss its beauty and stability because we are in our thinking minds so much. The topic of "forest bathing" intrigues me, and these authors have inspired me to spend more time in nature to find calm and clarity.

A teacher at a yoga retreat first introduced me to the work of **Dr. Qing Li** and the Japanese art of shinrin-yoku, which means *forest bathing.* I had never heard the term before and wanted to learn more. Read the forest bathing article linked on the companion website at resources.corwin.com/TeachingWithLight to learn about the highlights of this natural process of healing and finding inspiration in nature.

As I learned more about forest bathing, I discovered another book titled *The Healing Magic of Forest Bathing: Finding Calm, Creativity, and Connection in the Natural World* by **Julia Plevin** (2019). I enrolled in one of Julia's courses for entrepreneurs who want to contribute to the greater community. The Tree Ring Circle course supported me in evolving my idea for a Teacher Legacy Network. Learn more about Julia's work at www.forestbathing.club. Now I intentionally create time in nature and use my natural surroundings to keep me balanced and creative.

FEEL Inspiration. I first became acquainted with Jon Kabat-Zinn when I purchased his book, *Wherever You Go, There You Are* (1994). The title reminded me that I cannot hide from my feelings.

INSTEAD OF SAYING "LET IT GO" WE SHOULD PROBABLY SAY "LET IT BE."

—JON KABAT-ZINN

7

Be the
Wave

Go with
the flow.

Life Is Easy When I Am in the Flow

 Podcast Introduction to the Chapter

We all have changes and transitions in our lives, and some of them may be more challenging than others. Whether we are moving to a new city, having a baby, starting a new job, or retiring after a long career, each change brings both excitement and uncertainty. Changes can bring up deep emotions that influence our decision-making process. Our behaviors and responses influence all the people around us. Sometimes change can paralyze us and prevent us from doing anything. Change can also influence our ability to move forward, and it may impact our relationships with our family, friends, and colleagues.

Going with the flow of life is a lot harder than it sounds. The dynamics of an organization or family may not allow us to hide under the covers like we may want to! Sometimes we try to hold on and keep our lives the same as they were in the past. Other times we may try to take attention away from ourselves. My friend used to call it *staying under the radar*. This meant don't make waves or bring any attention to yourself. This is not an easy task for me since I like to speak up, ask questions, and share ideas, which can lead to making lots of waves.

What I have learned is that when I am in the flow of my life, *being the wave*, everything seems so much easier. I am in the present moment, and there is no effort to stop something from happening or to control the outcome of a situation. Most changes bring ups and downs that need to be addressed, and like waves, sometimes they are very steep and sometimes they are calm.

In this chapter you will explore your own life transitions and changes that may have impacted you physically and emotionally. This is an opportunity to reflect on what you learned and how you can continue to intentionally apply your lessons as you move forward.

Wisdom Through Stories

My Story—Changing Perspective: Directing to Accepting

Audio Reading by the Author

This is a story about a time in my life when I had to make a decision to stay or move on. I had been working successfully at a city university leading a student teaching program. It was rewarding and fulfilling, and it provided me with many opportunities to express my ideas creatively. But I had received a new offer for a job that was closer to home, offered a retirement package, and was an exciting start-up project funded by a federal grant. On face value the change to a new position would be a good one for me.

When I look back, the decision to accept the new offer clearly was the right one for me. However, at the time, it caused much anxiety and made me question myself. The anxiety affected me physically and emotionally. It led to hives and chest pains as well as emotional feelings, which often exhibited themselves as tears. I questioned my intuition and wondered if this was the one time that following my heart might not be the right decision. How did I put myself in this place of uncertainty and emotional turmoil?

In the job interview, the executive director explained the hierarchy at this public university and the many layers of directors and administrators. She asked, "Coming from directing your own program at a prestigious private university overseeing more than 25 team members, can you transition to becoming a member of the team?" The question made me pause. I hadn't thought about that. Then I said, "Yes, of course! In fact," I added, "I think it will be a refreshing change from being the person totally responsible for all the issues in the office, and I welcome the opportunity to step back from all the headaches."

Unfortunately, when I started the job, I noticed I still wanted to be the boss, the leader overseeing everything. So the transitional months were full of upset, tears, and hives. My husband listened and one day offered his advice. We happened to be on vacation swimming in the ocean at the time and he said, "Carol, be the wave." At that moment I let the waves take my body up and down. I felt the water, the sun, and the release of my anxiety when I just let go. It felt so good! As I continued to transition through that first year in this new role, I saw myself in the ocean water being the wave. That personal, physical experience was the beginning of my shift in perspective.

I also took some purposeful actions. You may find these three ideas useful in any change or transition you are facing.

- FOCUS ON THE WORK—Instead of looking at what was out of my control, I created ways to launch my new program. I needed to take the vision of a grant proposal and translate it into a workable program that recruited, prepared, and supported novice teachers and their mentors.

- LISTEN MORE, TALK LESS—I wasn't leading meetings anymore, so I needed to contribute in other ways by being a member of a team instead of directing the team.

- RESOLVE PRACTICAL ISSUES—Because I was easily distracted by the open work space I needed to be creative about where I could focus. After talking with the executive director, we agreed that I could work in one of the private rooms.

It took me more than a year to emotionally transition and accept my new role. Much like a first-year teacher, I learned that the second year is so much better. Riding that wave with its ups and downs allowed me to not only fulfill the vision of the program, it showed me that I could still be a leader when I wasn't the boss.

Another Teacher's Story

Meet Hydie Pettinger and listen to her story, *I will survive!*

Finding Your Wisdom: What's Your Story? What is your experience of change?

Reflect and respond to the following prompts:

1. When have you experienced a great change in your life? How did you respond?

2. How does my story of transitioning from *directing to accepting* relate to you?

3. How does the expression *be the wave* make you feel?

4. How do you take purposeful actions to make yourself feel more balanced through transitions?

5. What have you learned about yourself as you reflect on times of change and transition in your life and work?

FOCUS ON CHANGE

To change is to "make or become different, arrive at a fresh phase or become new" (Meriam-Webster, n.d.). Often the changes we experience come to us from others: a new boss, a new student, or a change in a classroom location. Sometimes we initiate the change, like I did when I chose to leave one position for another. Change can be revitalizing, and it can also paralyze us.

Our response to change can affect our body, mind, and spirit. We control our perspective, and that is what influences our health and well-being.

ASSESS YOUR HEALTH AND WELLNESS

Rate yourself from 1 to 3 (1 never think about it – 2 sometimes pay attention – 3 very mindful)

1. I eat healthy foods regularly.

    ① ② ③

2. I move my body intentionally (take the stairs, park away from the building, walk to the park, etc.).

    ① ② ③

3. My sleep routine is healthy.

    ① ② ③

4. Free time is scheduled into my week.

    ① ② ③

5. I resolve issues by going to the person who can do something about it.

    ① ② ③

What is the message you see in your responses?

PRACTICE SELF-CARE

PARTICIPATE—One way to participate is to be part of a group activity. Participating in a group or with one other person takes planning and coordination. When I walked with my friend Carol, we had to make a plan, and if we added another person, the scheduling became more complicated. For this self-care challenge let's stretch to participate in a group, especially if that is something you usually avoid.

TRY THIS!—Choose a group activity that will support your health and wellness. Walking? Running? Biking? Prayer? Art? Meditation? Dance? When we get stuck and unmotivated and are in the middle of a change or transition it is healthy to look outside of ourselves and reach out to others. We spend a lot of time alone as teachers.

I remember the first time I meditated with a group of people. I attended a class, and I found it challenging to sit and keep my mind quiet. I admit I did peek to see what everyone was doing. I learned that group energy is powerful and now will seek out opportunities to participate in groups for fun activities.

EXPLORE MINDFUL RESOURCES

Links to these books and the authors' websites are available at resources.corwin.com/Teaching WithLight.

What we eat, how we eat, and when we eat relates to our physical and mental health.

Two of my favorite cookbooks are *The Mystic Cookbook* by Denise and Meadow Linn (2012) and a recent new find for me *The Lotus Kitchen* by Skip Jennings and Gwen Kenneally (2015). These books bring an artistic flair to cooking and presenting meals in unique ways.

REMEMBER What Will Support You

- Reflect on times in your life when you experienced great change, and acknowledge what you did to support yourself.

- When there are things you cannot control, focus on your work and be creative about how you can contribute.

- Listen more and take in the comments from those around you without judging them.

- Solve the solvable problems that are within your control and the situations that can improve the day-to-day challenges in your work day. When you have a problem talk to the person who can do something about it.

- Go with the flow, and allow your body, mind, and spirit to release all that anxiety that no longer serves you. Be the wave!

Be Inspired by the Words of Others

LISTEN to Inspiring Leaders

LEARN About Influential Authors and Books

Meet Caitlin Krause and listen to her message of how to be the wave.

Be the wave reminds me that when I go with the flow, instead of against the current, I find my life moving more smoothly. When I use these short inspirational messages daily it starts the day intentionally and positively. More information is available on the companion website at resources.corwin.com/TeachingWithLight.

I was introduced to **Lao Tzu**'s work through *The Tao of Leadership*. This version written by **John Heider** (2014) was given to me as a gift when I was preparing for a new role as the teachers' union president. The short, thoughtful passages grounded me before meetings, prepared me for my day, and inspired me to go with the flow. I usually just open to a random page, read the message, and consider it the right thing for me to pay attention to at that moment in time. Now in its ninth printing, this book continues to offer insight to me.

Pema Chödrön's books also provide me with comfort and common sense to keep me flowing and accepting what is going on in my life. The first book I read, *Start Where You Are: A Guide to Compassionate Living* (2001), helped me stay positive during some tough personal challenges. Her new book, *Welcoming the Unwelcome: Wholehearted Living in a Brokenhearted World* (2019), brings a timely message to all of us today. I have many of her books on my shelf, and I refer to them when I need a reminder to be the wave.

FEEL Inspiration. I was introduced to Buckminster "Bucky" Fuller when I found an article titled, "The Anticipatory Leader: Buckminster Fuller's Principles for Making the World Work" (Gabel & Walker, 2006). Design Principle #5 was "Be a 'Trim Tab,'" and this variation is chiseled on his gravestone.

CALL ME TRIM TAB.

—BUCKY FULLER

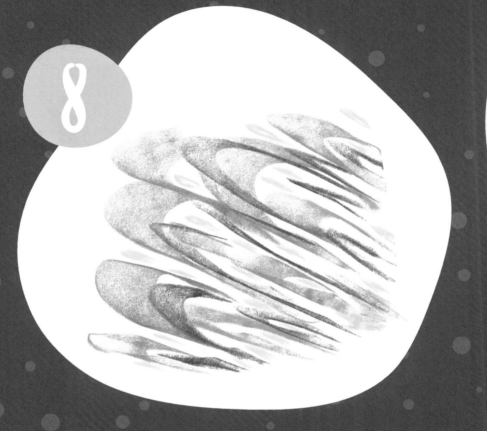

8

Always
Be Brave

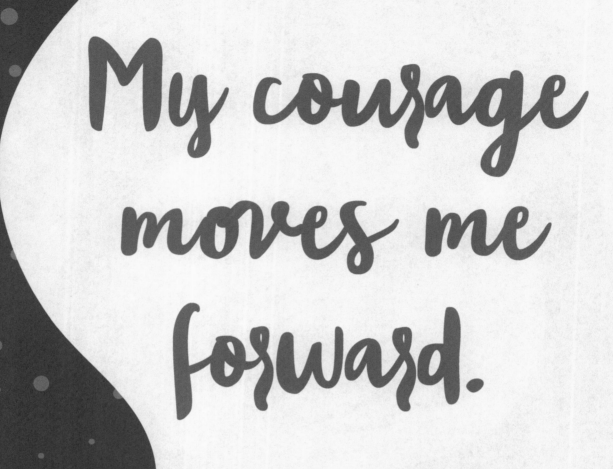

My courage moves me forward.

Going Beyond the Classroom: Teacher Leadership

 Podcast Introduction to the Chapter

Teacher leadership takes many forms. The teacher leader role can be as complicated as organizing a professional event over several months or as simple as sharing an idea at a faculty meeting. Most teacher leadership roles find us in charge of one of the many committees required to complete the day-to-day operations in schools.

Teacher leadership roles can also emerge from a teacher's own interests and skills. The leadership roles offered through professional organizations and teachers' unions bring teachers to district, state, national, and even international audiences. These roles often relate to the mission of the educational organization and teachers who choose to become members of these groups do so because the principles align with their beliefs and values.

It takes time, commitment, and courage to participate in a professional organization in addition to the regular duties of a teacher. When we step into a public discussion of policies and procedures we put ourselves in the realm of administration. This may open us to criticism from our colleagues or parents. Our participation makes us vulnerable, especially if we take an unpopular position on any issue.

I believe in teacher leadership. I know it is a challenging role for many of us, because teaching in our own classrooms with our students is more intimate and rewarding. Fear often holds us back from stepping out of our classrooms to participate in larger organizations. We question: What will other teachers think? Do I have anything to contribute? Will it make a difference?

In this chapter you will reflect on your teacher leadership opportunities and desires. Will your participation beyond your classroom contribute to the greater good of the profession and ultimately to more students? Is fear stopping you from taking that first step?

Wisdom Through Stories

My Story—Do I Really Want to Lead?

Audio Reading by the Author

There was a time in my life when I was shy. No one believes that is true, because I can be very outspoken. As a child I read a lot and played by myself in my own fantasy world. I had a few close friends, but I felt insecure and was not forthcoming with my ideas. Even though I was the oldest in my family, as a female, I felt my voice was not as strong as my younger brother's, who was more dominant in voice and action. When I began my career as a teacher I kept to myself and my close friends, who were also my colleagues. I focused on my dream of teaching in my own classroom and was totally engaged with the daily tasks of a teacher.

After several years, I felt the desire to stretch a bit more and take some risks such as speaking at a faculty meeting or sharing ideas with colleagues who were not my close friends. These new relationships broadened my circle and gave me more confidence. I decided to participate on more teacher committees, which led me to representing my school as a union representative. I enjoyed bringing ideas forward to union leaders but noticed they were not embraced by the current leadership. I decided to seek a position as vice president in the local teachers' union so I could bring new ideas forward. Having never run for an elected office before, I was a bit nervous. At the time, the officers in the union were all men from the high school, and I was a female elementary school teacher.

Long story short, I did not win. My colleagues later shared that they didn't think I wanted to win! I hadn't asked for their votes or shared my campaign ideas. All I did was put my name on the ballot—a rookie move for sure. The next year, I decided to try again, and it turned out quite differently. The candidate for president withdrew from the election at the last minute, and I had the largest number of votes for vice president. The committee asked me to serve as president! I was not prepared for that! With my knees shaking and my heart pounding, I stood before the preK–12 teachers and publicly stepped into the role of president, promising to represent all teachers in the district to the best of my ability. It was thrilling and scary at the same time.

Three things I did to acknowledge that I was stepping into a teacher leader role may be useful to you.

- ASK PEOPLE FOR SUPPORT—I learned that I needed to share my ideas and ask for support. If I wanted to win and have people vote for me, I couldn't take their support for granted.

- REFLECT ON MY INTENTION—When I lost the first election, I had a year to think about how I specifically wanted to contribute to education. I had time to think about my campaign ideals and the way I would present myself as a leader.

- ACCEPT THE NEW ROLE—Some things happen for a reason. I did not run for president, and yet there I was in the position with the most votes. I could have said no. I chose to say yes, and I truly accepted this as a learning opportunity.

I served in the role for 2 years, and I learned more about representing teachers' voices than in any other role in my life. It took courage initially to take that first step to put my name on the ballot and then to run again the next year after I lost. I am proud to say I was able to bring many new ideas forward including ways to collaborate with the school board. This experience also demonstrated that an elementary school female could successfully lead the teachers' union. This memory reminds me to *always be brave*.

Meet Takeru "TK" Nagayoshi and listen to his story, *Teachers Voices Matter.*

Finding Your Wisdom: What's Your Story?

Reflect and respond to the following prompts:

1. How does my message and my story relate to your experience of being brave?
2. Have you sought out teacher leadership roles in your school? Explain.
3. If you have never been a teacher leader, what is stopping you?
4. How do you think teacher leadership contributes to the school and district?
5. Are you a member of a professional organization or union? If yes, share your experience. If no, why are you not a member of any education groups?

Mindful
Living
Actions

FOCUS ON FUN

Being brave doesn't mean we exclude fun from our lives. As teachers we often get so serious about our work and its importance that we take things personally. When we can laugh at ourselves it releases tension. A sense of humor should be a requirement for any teacher!

Teacher leaders are often in the spotlight and are easy targets to make fun of. Sometimes their personal traits and characteristics make it easy to laugh at them. This is NOT the type of fun I am talking about. It is not about making fun of someone. In fact, these types of behaviors keep us from participating as a leader, because we are afraid someone will talk about us like that, too.

ASSESS YOUR RELATIONSHIPS

Rate yourself from 1 to 3 (1 disagree – 2 sometimes – 3 agree)

1. I intentionally surround myself with positive people.
   ① ② ③

2. Teachers like to be around me.
   ① ② ③

3. I have a sense of humor and like to laugh.
   ① ② ③

4. I am a contributing member on school and district committees.
   ① ② ③

5. People would describe me as easy to get along with.
   ① ② ③

What is the message you see in your responses?

PRACTICE SELF-CARE

PLAY—Having a relationship with yourself is an important and healthy way to have fun. In Julia Cameron's book (2016), *The Artist's Way*, you have to commit to an artist date with yourself each week. Cameron describes an artist date as assigned play dates. It is a solo activity to explore something that interests you. It doesn't have to be anything artistic, just something that sounds like fun!

I remember reading Julia's book and planning these weekly dates. It was hard for me to assign myself a *fun* activity that was solo. I said to myself, "I have to do this every week?" It actually got easier; I explored so many new places, and there were times I just sat at a coffee shop alone reading a book.

TRY THIS!—Plan a play date with yourself. What would be really fun for you to do alone? Select something that you don't already do. Stretch yourself to explore new places or activities. Choose a day and time to go outside of your home and commit to a time period for your date with yourself. Be Curious! Have fun!

EXPLORE MINDFUL RESOURCES

The links to these yoga teachers' websites are available at resources.corwin.com/Teaching WithLight.

I first met Megha Buttenheim (2016) at a weekend dance yoga retreat, which was part of my *Kind Yoga* (https://kindyogacom/) teacher training program with Diane Kovanda (2016). These powerful and inspiring women offer us their books, their joy, their inspiration, and lots of laughter!

REMEMBER What Will Support You

- Ask for support to achieve your goals. Don't take it for granted.

- Reflect on your intention for pursuing a teacher leadership role. Is it to serve the greater good?

- If a bigger role comes to you, reflect and accept. See how this fits into your learning as a leader.

- Vulnerability, courage, and bravery emerge as we represent others' voices.

- A sense of humor, fun, and play allow us to experience leadership in healthy ways.

Be Inspired by the Words of Others

LISTEN to Inspiring Leaders

LEARN About Influential Authors and Books

Meet Tiffany Green and listen to her experiences of being brave.

Always be brave reminds us that when it is time to speak our truth we must have the courage to do so. These two vibrant women have captured my attention and given me the courage to acknowledge my gifts and articulate my ideas. More information is available on the companion website at resources.corwin.com/TeachingWithLight.

I was first introduced to **Kelly McGonigal** when I attended a mentoring conference workshop in California. Her TED Talk and book *The Upside of Stress* (2016) are part of my courses because she shows us that life will have stress, and we can survive it and sometimes use it to thrive.

Kristen Lee and I met when I reached out to her to lead a workshop for stressed out teachers. Her business card workshop was titled *Helping Helpers*, and I knew her approach would be perfect for the aspiring teachers in my cohort. Her first book *Reset: Make the Most of Your Stress* (Lee, 2014) teaches us all how to pause and regroup before we act. She brings courage, beauty, and practical applications to her work. She encourages me to continue to be brave.

FEEL Inspiration. I remember feeling goose bumps when I first read this poem, *Our Deepest Fear*. A friend framed this excerpt from the poem and gave it to me as a gift. I encourage you to read the entire poem to see how the message relates to you.

OUR DEEPEST FEAR IS NOT THAT WE ARE INADEQUATE,

OUR DEEPEST FEAR IS THAT WE ARE POWERFUL BEYOND MEASURE,

IT IS OUR LIGHT, NOT OUR DARKNESS

THAT MOST FRIGHTENS US.

—MARIANNE WILLIAMSON

9

Dream Out Loud

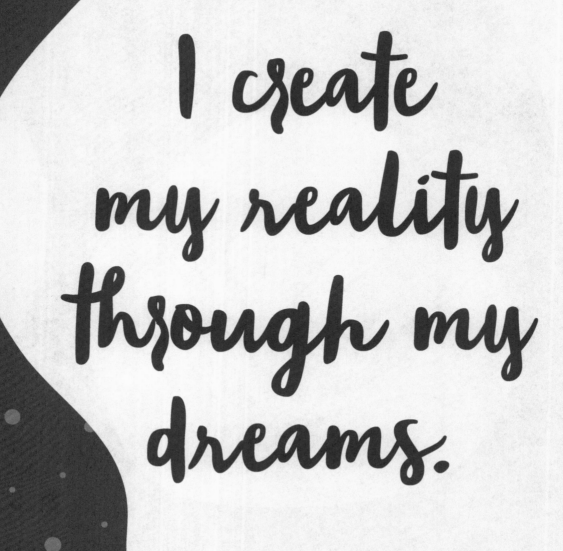

I create my reality through my dreams.

We Create What We Love

 Podcast Introduction to the Chapter

I believe we are all creative beings. When we spend too much time in our heads we miss seeing what we love and our dreams can become goals that are disconnected from our hearts. As a child, when I dreamed I would become a teacher I saw myself in my own classroom. The bubble was temporarily burst when my counselor said that this dream may not become a reality for me. I had to purposefully act to bring that dream to fruition, because I felt the love of this profession deep inside of me and I was not going to let it go. Finding our dreams takes stillness and listening. Realizing our dreams takes motivation, persistence, and action.

Throughout my career I have loved creating new ways to teach and motivate audiences. I always begin my dreaming process by asking myself the question, "What's missing?" and then I listen. The seed of any dream starts from that place of creation inside of us. Each and every one of us has the potential to *dream out loud* and share our ideas with others. We don't have to create all the ideas and dreams ourselves. Let's find the dreamers in our midst and support their dreams, too. As much as I love creating and implementing visions, I appreciate being part of a group that develops a dream I can get behind. I do love leading, no question about that, but I also love supporting leaders with vision.

Every time I create something new, whether it is a new way to deliver a lesson, or a strategy for teaching, I feel a sense of renewal. We have heard the saying, "If it isn't broken, don't fix it." Fixing is an opportunity to bring our creative powers to our teaching. Fixing isn't a bad thing.

In this chapter you will have the opportunity to uncover your dreams and choose one to move forward. Dreams can become realities if we choose the actions that align with our skills and gifts. Loving what we do has a whole lot of power in making a dream come true.

Wisdom Through Stories

My Story—Supporting Teacher Development

Audio Reading
by the Author

After about 10 years of teaching, I welcomed a student teacher into my classroom. I enjoyed sharing ideas, supervising lessons, and mentoring this beginner. I wanted to be sure I was modeling best practices and providing her with the best experience possible, so I spent my planning time reviewing my lessons to ensure she observed effective teaching.

Other teachers in the school were also hosting student teachers, and of course everyone talks about their experiences in the teachers' room. As I listened to the comments about what we were supposed to be doing with a student teacher, I asked myself my usual question, "What's missing here?" and my response was "A handbook for the cooperating teacher!" The college provided a list of rules and responsibilities along with required paperwork, but it didn't include actual day-to-day ideas for mentoring.

A state grant for classroom teachers offered me the opportunity to write a handbook, *So You're Going to Be a Cooperating Teacher*. The book led to the development of a district program called *Bridging the Gap*, where we provided information and support to all student teachers and their cooperating teachers. Another state grant gave me the opportunity to share the *Bridging the Gap* model with universities across the state. This experience sparked my enthusiasm for the possibilities of enhancing teacher preparation programs. I had discovered a new passion and a love beyond my own classroom. When the federal *Christa McAuliffe Fellowship Program* offered me an opportunity to intern at the Harvard Graduate School of Education, I knew I was on a new path.

During the internship, I was encouraged to apply to the doctoral program, and then the real adventure started. The year before I completed the doctoral program and my dissertation, I was offered a position in a teacher education program at a city university. I needed to reflect and ask myself, is this really what I want? I had been comfortable sharing my ideas with education faculty who partnered with my district, but could I actually lead a student teaching program at an unfamiliar university?

I thought about my decision in these ways, and you may find them useful to you if you are shifting from one dream to another.

- TALK WITH FRIENDS AND FAMILY— Take time to discuss what this new dream will look like in day-to-day reality. This means the details: How far is the commute, what are the work hours, and how do the operations of my life get handled? What am I leaving?

- ACKNOWLEDGE THE SYNCHRONICITIES—I always say there are no accidents. When doors open, I need to look at what is coming to me and see how these opportunities are aligned with my dreams.

- TRY IT OUT—Review your options. Can you test out the new role to see if it is really as good as it sounds? I had the option to take a leave of absence from my classroom for a full year before I made the commitment to accept the new position.

Dreaming out loud may sound crazy to some of your friends and family. But in the end it was me who had to make the decision. I had dreamed of helping novice teachers and their cooperating teachers, but never in my wildest dreams did I see myself in a leadership role at a university!

This rebirth of myself as a *teacher of teachers* renewed my passion and purpose to influence future generations of teachers. I had shared many of my ideas, and now I was presented with an opportunity to implement my vision in another way. Be careful what you wish for. It just might come to you when you dream out loud.

Another Teacher's Story

Meet Gerard Haskins and listen to his story, *I Want to Give Back.*

Finding your Wisdom: What's Your Story?—What are you dreaming about?

Reflect and respond to the following prompts:

1. How does the message and the story in this chapter relate to you?
2. What are some of your dreams for enhancing education? Think big!
3. Which dream would you actually like to make happen now?
4. List three skills and qualities you bring that can make this dream a reality.
5. How does your dream relate to your current role?

FOCUS ON RENEWAL

We all need a break sometimes. Most teachers would say they are so busy, busy, busy that there is just not any time for a break. Renewal is a time for us to decompress and reflect on what is working and what isn't meeting our needs. Most of us hesitate to take that time, fearing we will never catch up if we stop. Renewing allows us to dream and pull our heads up from the daily tasks to see what is going on around us. We can't really think big if we are constantly *doing* and not stepping away to just be in the moment. Our dreams can't emerge if they are so buried we can't find them.

ASSESS YOUR CREATIVITY

Rate yourself from 1 to 3 (1 almost never – 2 sometimes – 3 always)

1. I listen to my inner voice regularly.
   ① ② ③

2. My creative ideas are written down so I can refer to them.
   ① ② ③

3. I create solutions to problems in my classroom and school.
   ① ② ③

4. I consider myself a creative and innovative person.
   ① ② ③

5. Creativity is a way for me to express myself.
   ① ② ③

What is the message you see in your responses?

PRACTICE SELF-CARE

CREATE—To create our dreams and put them into action, we first need to understand what creativity means. I do *not* mean your artistic ability to draw or paint. This is not the creativity we are exploring. I mean your ability to turn imaginative ideas into reality in your schools or to create an experience for yourself that is enjoyable. Dreaming out loud requires sharing with others because you need buy-in to implement your idea. This is a risk. Many of my projects started with creative reflection processes looking for hidden patterns. My goal was to generate solutions to current problems teachers were facing. I believe we are all creative. Creativity does not have to always be about innovation and solving a problem. It can be a personal experience that you enjoy.

TRY THIS!—Discover or revisit an activity you enjoy. What type of experiences are you drawn to? Creativity is not about being perfect. It is not about professional artistry; it is about being in the moment enjoying something you choose to do for yourself. Dedicate 30 minutes to doing something you love. I love creating abstract art with pastels because they are messy and colorful. What is calling you?

EXPLORE MINDFUL RESOURCES

Links to both of these resources are available at resources.corwin.com/TeachingWithLight.

I completed the Sweet Dreams Project from the Inspiredideas.me website a few years ago. Maria Clark encouraged me to think big and conceptualize my life's purpose. Cameron Marzelli's resources, offered on the Stillwoman.com website, focus our intention on what matters most to us.

REMEMBER What Will Support You

- Recognize the doors that open to you, and intentionally decide if they align with your vision and values.

- Talk honestly about the details that relate to dreaming out loud and putting any vision into action. Make sure you actually want to do this.

- Test the vision out before you commit to it. Make sure the dream actually is as good as you think it is.

- Accept the comments of others who may not see the vision the way you do. Don't take them personally. Use their feedback to modify your dreams as you move forward.

- Collaborate and support the dreams and visions of others. Acknowledge inspiring leaders around you.

Be Inspired by the Words of Others

LISTEN to Inspiring Leaders

LEARN About Influential Authors and Books

Meet Lily Sanabria and listen to the ways she dreams out loud.

Dreaming out loud can be scary, especially if other people don't agree with our dreams. This makes us vulnerable and at risk of retreating from the ideas we wish to offer. These two very different authors allowed me to dream and reach for the stars. More information is available on the companion website at resources.corwin.com/TeachingWithLight.

Brené Brown rocked our world with her TED Talk and her book *Daring Greatly: How the Courage to be Vulnerable Transforms the Way We Live, Love, Parent, and Lead* (2015). Brown talks about feelings and thoughts we would never share with anyone. She created space for us to not only be vulnerable but to see our vulnerability as a strength that keeps us authentic and allows us to fulfill our dreams.

A book I have had on my shelf for decades is by **Shakti Gawain**, *Creative Visualization: Use the Power of Your Imagination to Create What You Want in Your Life* (1974/2016). I remember when I first read this book thinking that is was magic. Shakti shares simple and practical ways to use affirmations, heal our bodies and minds, and clear negative thoughts. If we want to dream big and create a positive life this book is a timeless process to embrace.

FEEL Inspiration. I met Roland S. Barth on my 40th birthday. He had a profound influence on my teaching because his work recognizes the value of teachers' dreams. In his book *Improving Schools from Within* (1990) he encourages us to have a vision.

I LEARNED THAT EACH OF US MUST HAVE A VISION . . .

IT CAN ACT AS A GUIDING BEACON ONLY AS LONG AS I HOLD IT IN FRONT OF ME.

—ROLAND S. BARTH

10

Pay It Forward

Looking Back and Leaning Forward

 Podcast Introduction to the Chapter

My career has been amazing. I followed my heart into teaching, learned to bloom where I was planted, shared my light, accepted things as they were, felt the wave, faced the sun when times were dark, was brave, dreamed, rippled, and now it is time for me to pay it forward. I began my journey in an elementary classroom, transitioned to higher education designing teacher preparation practicum programs, and now I lead a dedicated group of teacher leaders in my own company. My life has been full, and my desire to share what I have learned with others has now become a focus for me.

When I formally completed my work at the university, the word *retirement* didn't reflect what I was feeling. I wasn't ready to retire. At about that same time, I had the opportunity to hear the famous poet, Mary Oliver, read her poem titled *The Summer Day* (1992). As I sat in a packed auditorium on a summer evening with all Mary's admirers, I felt chills through my body when she read the last line, "Tell me what is it you plan to do with your one wild and precious life?" At that moment I wasn't sure, but I knew I would continue on my teacher journey.

Later on, the expression *pay it forward* came to me, and I felt a sense of purpose in knowing I could support the success of novice teachers in some small way by sharing what I had learned. That is how I came to build a company with the mission to transform education for students by supporting novice teachers and their mentors.

One of the saddest things about U.S. education is that the wisdom of our most successful teachers is lost to the profession when they retire.

—John Dewey

Parker Palmer's book, *On the Brink of Everything* (2018), inspired me to think about the wisdom of our retired teachers in a new way. He shares his thoughts in essays titled "The Dance of the Generations" and "The Music of Mentoring." Parker writes that it is time to release the metaphor of "passing the baton" to the young and instead embrace a more fulfilling model of mentoring where young and old mutually share their talents with the world. I believe it is time to formally and systematically include post-service opportunities for our retired teachers in our districts and professional organizations. Building on our pre-service and in-service models, we must add a *continuing* service phase to our education continuum to capture the success stories, the wisdom, and the joy of teaching from our retired colleagues. This generational mentoring process will benefit all involved in the success of students.

In this closing chapter you will have an opportunity to assess where you are on the continuum of your teaching career. What are you *leaning toward*? How does your one precious life relate to you paying it forward from where you are right now? How can you honor the legacy of retired teachers? Use this time to find your wisdom and your light. Trust the process.

Wisdom Through Stories

My Story—Reflect. Recruit. Redirect. Repeat!

Audio Reading by the Author

When I made the decision to formally retire from the university, I thought I would be teaching one course part time. I didn't want to be *that professor* who just couldn't let go of teaching, but I just wasn't sure about my next steps yet. This is the same time period when I enrolled in a yoga teacher training program. I wanted to learn yoga poses more systematically, and I didn't want to hurt myself in any yoga classes. Now I had time.

As it turned out, teaching the course at the university didn't work out, and that allowed me to get more deeply involved in my yoga teacher program. The training expanded my thinking and opened my heart. The meditation practices gave me more clarity and revealed my inner voice. This in turn opened me up to *being curious*, which allowed my abstract pastel art images to emerge. The training also led me to think about how mindfulness and mentoring are connected.

I was in this yoga mindset when I attended a conference on the topic of social-emotional learning. I sat next to a colleague, Janet, who I knew informally from other conferences. She was familiar with my academic work, and she asked what I planned to do now that I was formally retired from the university. This of course is the expected and typical question most people ask when you leave. I am sure I mumbled something like "I don't know for sure." Then she asked a deeper question, "What do you wish you could do?" Without hesitation I responded, "I wish I could offer graduate courses for mentors online." Where did that idea come from? How would I even begin? Janet responded, "I can help you with that!" So I said to myself, "Why not?"

Even though I am formally retired, I am not too tired to be inspired! I continue to offer courses and free resources to mentors and novice teachers and I continue to create new ideas. My current interest is to create a *Legacy Teacher Network* for retired teachers who still want to contribute to education and the future generations of teachers.

You may consider these steps if you find yourself with a big idea and want to pay it forward.

- REFLECT—I took some soul searching time and asked myself, "Do I really want to start my own business?" I had always worked for someone else. I would have to create the infrastructure myself from the ground up. I gave it a try and became an entrepreneur, creating Mentoring in Action.

- RECRUIT—I knew I did not want to work alone. The good news was I had a team of people who worked on my previous university projects who were now available. They all agreed to move ahead with me!

- REDIRECT—Redirecting my energy from one of a *retiree* mindset to *entrepreneur* was revitalizing for me! I always have loved start-up projects where I can create and imagine new ways of doing things. This felt good.

- REPEAT—I *reflect* each semester to see if I want to continue offering courses or adding new ones. I check in with my team and *recruit* new members if needed for special projects, and I *redirect* my energy and the focus of Mentoring in Action to engage in current issues as needed.

I am proud to report we have successfully completed our fifth year as a small business offering resources to novice teachers and their mentors! Mentoring in Action has been an integral part of my legacy to *pay it forward*.

Another Teacher's Story

Meet Megan Sobol-Flowers and listen to her story, *Mentoring Matters!*

Finding Your Wisdom: What's Your Story?—How will you pay it forward?

Reflect and respond to the following prompts:

1. How does my message about retiring or redirecting your energy relate to you?
2. What does *pay it forward* mean to you?
3. How have you demonstrated your commitment to teaching?
4. What do you love about being a teacher?
5. What is your plan for your one wild and precious career as a teacher?

FOCUS ON DEVOTION

Devotion requires us to demonstrate our loyalty and dedication to a cause. My cause has been to be a teacher. It is a choice I made early in my life, and I have never regretted it. For me the word devotion is associated with inspiration and is reflected by our inspired actions; actions that engage us in a creative process of teaching. The internal flame—or the "fire in the belly," as one of my colleagues described it—is the inner passion that keeps us teaching. It is our inspiration, excitement, and breath that keeps us on the teaching path. Only we can feel our devotion to the path of being a teacher. Our students and colleagues can see our love of teaching demonstrated in our words and our actions inside and outside the classroom. We can empower others and pay it forward as educators by being the best version of ourselves.

ASSESS YOUR BELIEFS

Rate yourself from 1to 3 (1 disagree – 2 sometimes – 3 agree)

1. I am committed to teaching.
   ① ② ③

2. My love for teaching is demonstrated in my actions.
   ① ② ③

3. I honor experienced teachers and their contributions.
   ① ② ③

4. My teaching brings me joy.
   ① ② ③

5. I am inspired to create something new to support others.
   ① ② ③

What is the message you see in your responses?

PRACTICE SELF-CARE

CARE, COMPASSION, AND LOVE—Someone once said to me, "When you do what you love, you will love what you do." I have loved and continue to love all the experiences that being a teacher have presented to me. Love is defined in many ways: attachment, devotion, admiration for, and enthusiasm come to mind. I also would include caring about our students, their families, and our school community as we as teachers bring compassion to our work.

TRY THIS!—Mentor a teacher! You choose someone who you know would benefit from your support, caring, and compassionate listening. Remember all the people who helped you and inspired you? If you can't think of anyone who helped you then YOU get to begin the cycle of mentoring as you pay it forward. You know who needs you now. Share what you love. Come from love. Encourage your mentee to find love in the everyday work of teaching. Use the resources offered on my website MentoringinAction.com to guide you.

EXPLORE MINDFUL RESOURCES

You can find links to these books at Resources .Corwin.Com/TeachingWithLight or by going to MentoringinAction.com.

I wrote *A Mindful Living Journal: Art and Affirmations to Nourish Your Soul* (Radford, 2019) and *Mindful Mentoring: A Guide for Mentors and Mentees* (Radford, 2019) because I wanted to share mindfulness with teachers and other audiences. These colorful journals offer us a place to reflect and integrate positive energy into our daily lives so we can bring the best version of ourselves to our work.

REMEMBER What Will Support You

- Reflect on what is most meaningful for you in your life and career right now. Take a deep dive into your inner voice. This is not a pros and cons reflection. This is soul searching.

- Recruit others to be part of your support team. Even if your project is solo we all need a team of people who believe in us. This keeps us honest and moving toward our goals.

- Redirect your energy and focus on what is in front of you now and don't look back. Stay in the present moment and experience what is going on around you so you can make informed decisions.

- Repeat the steps as often as you need to so you stay on your path. Just because your inner voice tells you this is the right way to go doesn't mean it is easy. Focus on your vision.

- Pay it forward because you care for the profession and you want the next generation of teachers to be successful, joyful, and loving teachers.

Be Inspired by the Words of Others

LISTEN to Inspiring Leaders

LEARN About Influential Authors and Books

Meet Kathleen Dunne Gagne and listen to how she continues to pay it forward.

Pay it forward from a place of generosity and abundance. These last two authors guide us in thinking about what we share, why we share it, and how we pay it forward. To learn more about these authors, visit the companion website at resources.corwin.com/TeachingWithLight.

When I read the book *What's Worth Fighting For? Working Together for Your School* (Fullan & Hargreaves, 1992) I was still in the classroom and deciding about whether to take on some additional leadership roles. The book made me think about what I would stand for. Later, I met **Andy Hargreaves** and had the privilege of collaborating with him on a teacher leadership conference. His down to earth attitude and great humor were refreshing. His books *Sustainable Leadership* (Hargreaves & Fink, 2006) and *Collaborative Professionalism* (Hargreaves & O'Connor, 2018) offer us steps to sustain our ideas in a collaborative context of sharing and appreciation.

The Four Agreements (1997) by **Don Miguel Ruiz** helped me think about how I share my work with others. My friend Carol and I would repeat the agreements in our morning walks. When we couldn't remember one of them, we took it as a sign that it was the agreement we needed to pay attention to that day. What we have to share matters when it is offered with love and the intention to contribute to the greater good. An important part of illuminating our own teaching path requires us to light the way for those who come after us.

FEEL Inspiration. Sharon "Christa" McAuliffe was selected as the first teacher to travel into space. I watched with my students on the tragic day that the Challenger exploded on lift-off. Several years later, I had the honor of receiving a scholarship in her name. Her famous quote (Ainsworth, n.d.) reminds me . . .

I TOUCH THE FUTURE; I TEACH!

—SHARON "CHRISTA" MCAULIFFE

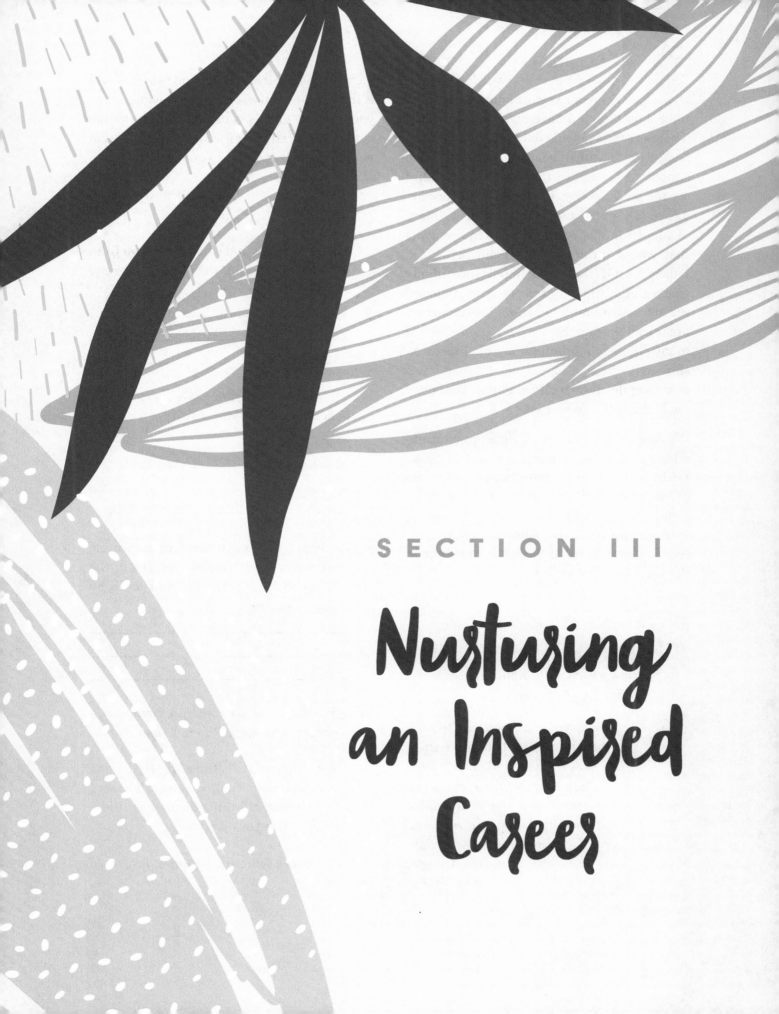

SECTION III

Nurturing
an Inspired
Career

When we choose to teach we don't think about it as a career. At least I didn't. I wanted to be a teacher and have my own classroom. That is as far as I looked. I didn't see the *profession* or the other people around me who supported my life in the classroom. I didn't see the public policy that would influence my day-to-day practice or the state department of education that implemented requirements that would influence how I did my work. I didn't understand the importance of my teacher education professors who prepared me to teach or how professional development organizations and the teachers' union related to my classroom. I didn't know that relationships with my colleagues, parents, and students would have such an impact on how I made decisions. Now I see.

We are part of an interconnected community where everything influences everything else. I believe our wisdom, our ability to take care of ourselves, and our openness to the inspiration from others will nurture us and in turn sustain us for the duration of our professional career. All of the roles contribute to the success of our students.

REVEALING YOUR WISDOM: WHAT DID YOU LEARN?

Review: View - *the ability to see something.* Re - *to do again.*

Read your responses to the questions listed at the end of the *Wisdom Through Stories.* Sometimes when we write responses to reflective prompts, patterns and themes emerge right away. Often though, we miss these messages as we are writing, and that is why it is important to take some time now to review your words. This is your opportunity to discover those hidden messages and to reveal your inner wisdom from your stories.

Respond to the following prompts to deepen your inquiry:

1. List two stories that stood out to you from *My Stories. How did these messages relate to you?*

   _____

   _____

   _____

2. Which of *Another Teacher's Story* podcasts touched your heart? Explain.

   _____

   _____

   _____

3. Review *Your Story* reflections for any of the prompts you completed in any of the lesson chapters. What did you learn by doing this process?

   _____

   _____

   _____

Revisit: Visit - *to see and spend time with (someone or something).* Re - *to do again.*

Take some time to revisit the *Mindful Living Actions* you chose to complete in each lesson. Spend some time thinking about how these actions influence your well-being.

Respond to the following prompts to deepen your inquiry:

1. Which *Focus* areas stood out to you as important? List your top three.

   _____

   _____

   _____

2. As you review all the *Assess* sections in each lesson what do you notice about your responses? Is there a common theme?

   _____

   _____

   _____

3. Did you have some favorites in the *Practice Self-care and Try This* sections? List your top two here.

   _____

   _____

   _____

Rethink: Think - to *use one's mind actively to form connected ideas.* Re - *to do again.*

Rethink the ideas that have emerged for you as you look back over the *Be Inspired By the Words of Others* section and notice what stood out as most inspiring to you. Are you making some connections to your own life?

Respond to the following prompts to deepen your inquiry:

1. List your top three inspiring quotes from the *Feel Inspiration* section featured at the end of each lesson.

   _____

   _____

   _____

2. Review the Ten Lessons and choose three authors or books you would like to read or learn more about from the *Learn About Influential Authors and Books* section. Which one will you read first?

   _____

   _____

   _____

3. Star or highlight one or two of the most important ideas in the *Remember* section for any of the Ten Lessons you read.

   _____

   _____

   _____

MAKING INSPIRED DECISIONS

At the beginning of the book in Section I you were asked, "What is your career intention?" I now ask, "Has your intention changed?" Setting an intention involves our emotions, our hearts, as well as our minds. I believe nurturing a career in teaching requires us to focus on what will fulfill us and contribute to the greater good. Setting an intention involves our emotions and our hearts. Our intentions lead us to our next steps. What do you actually intend for your one precious life?

As you look at the choices you have in front of you, reflect on what gives you joy in your career and life. Feeling joy is usually a good indicator that you are on the right path. Take some time to think about the path you are on right now. Is this the way you thought you would be going? *Teaching With Light* requires us to choose light. What *you* bring to teaching matters.

WHAT GIVES YOU JOY?

In Section I you were introduced to three questions that I have used frequently when talking with prospective teachers about their vocation. I would like to circle back to a modified version of those questions.

> What gives you joy in your teaching?
>
> What are your gifts and talents?
>
> How can you contribute to the teaching profession right now?

Joy nurtures us and sustains us on our teaching journey. Being able to experience the moments when we are in the flow also nurtures us. Acknowledging our gifts and talents and being willing to share them with others allows us to experience generosity. Because the needs of the profession are continually changing, we need to bring forth new ways of educating our students. To do this we must be courageous and creative. The solutions to the challenges we face need to come from within the profession, and that means we must find our way to contribute in ways that bring joy to our teaching.

FINDING YOUR TAO

*Tao (道; dào) literally means **way** but can also be interpreted as road, path, or doctrine.*

I was first introduced to the word Tao over 30 years ago when a dear friend gave me a book titled *The Tao of Leadership* (Heider, 2014). Inspired by Lao Tzu's teachings, these short messages translated into English became a daily source of inspiration for me. I often use this book to select a random reading and have given it as a gift to teachers.

My path has taken many turns, and I have changed my role several times from classroom teacher to teacher educator, project director, collaborator with the state department of education, and now to entrepreneur starting my own company. I always felt I was a teacher in each and every one of the roles. I will always identify as a teacher because I believe it is my path and purpose in life. This journey has always shown me that next small step. Sometimes I felt overwhelmed when I had to make a decision that would influence my life, and other times I was filled with happiness and excitement. Taking the step is what mattered. I trusted the path. I still do.

Success is every minute you live. It's the process of living. It's stopping for the moments of beauty, of pleasure; the moments of peace. Success is not a destination that you ever reach. Success is the quality of the journey.

—Jennifer James

As you reflect on the decisions you have made in the past or the choices you have in front of you on your path, I encourage you to do these three things:

Stay inspired—Build a community of support. Surround yourself with people who lift you up and offer you the guidance that brings out your gifts and talents. Read books that teach you new ways to look at things. Create your personal Circle of Mentors, which we learned about in Section I, and use them to guide you.

Take care of yourself—Maintain your balance. *You* are an important part of this education community. Make yourself the most important priority of each day. Embrace your health, discover your ability to maintain your balance, and see this as the ultimate gift to your students, your family, and your life. Be a positive role model. Self-care is not selfish!

Share your wisdom—Embrace your power. Together we have the power to be the change we all want to see in education. It takes each one of us looking inside to see what we know to be true. Your words, conversations, and stories matter. Share what you know with confidence, compassion, and courage.

CHOOSE LIGHT

So ultimately it is up to each one of us as individuals to choose how we want to present ourselves to our students, colleagues, and the larger educational community. Will we blame others for the challenges we face, or will we creatively propose ways to resolve the issues? Collectively we create a source of power, energy, and wisdom that cannot be ignored. When all teachers, no matter their role, unite we bring the light we are looking for into our classrooms, our communities, and the world.

I remember when my father died, some of his friends talked about how he lived life to the fullest. He was always very proud of me becoming a teacher and the first to graduate from college. He and my mother taught me the values of hard work, honesty, and being happy.

Family, food, and fun is our family motto, and we celebrate this often. This quote reminds me of my father, George, and it also expresses how I want to live my life.

I want to be thoroughly used up when I die, for the harder I work, the more I live. I rejoice in life for its own sake. Life is no "brief candle" to me. It is sort of a splendid torch which I have a hold of for the moment, and I want to make it burn as brightly as possible before handing it over to future generations.

—George Bernard Shaw

Being used up doesn't mean we work 24/7; it means we LIVE 24/7. How we choose to live our lives, go to school, take care of ourselves and others is up to us. I remember at a particularly hard time in my life, my father just simply asked, "Are you happy?" and when I heard myself say "No," I knew I had to do something about it. That of course is the hard part, the doing something about it—the making myself happy part. I believe to be happy we must make happiness one of our goals. We make ourselves happy by choosing experiences that fulfill us. When we are happy it opens gateways to new ways of being and creative ideas.

The Ten Lessons I have shared in this book are just a few of the many lessons I have learned along the way. They are just examples of the ways in which I learned how to respond, react, and move forward to the next phase along my teaching journey. I now understand that my mindset is crucial to nurturing me and sustaining my career as a teacher. Are you half empty or half full? Do you see an inspired career as possible?

Can you find joy as a teacher? Are you willing to look at your role in contributing to the greater good of the profession?

Life is not measured by how many breaths we take, but by the moments that take our breath away.

—Maya Angelou

As teachers our stories are reminders of those moments. I have had many breathtaking moments as a teacher. I believe it is our duty to remember the powerful moments we have experienced. Those moments of joy when we see a student read for the first time, or hope when a parent supports their child's learning, or bravery when our colleagues speak up and stand for an idea that is important to us all.

CLOSING THOUGHTS

As my stories emerged in these Ten Lessons, I saw that there were silver linings to each one. What I originally remembered as pain, I can now see as learning. As your stories emerge, notice if you are judging yourself and others or if you are listening to your inner voice with a compassionate heart. I encourage you to uncover your stories of resilience, strength, hope, humor, and optimism. These are the stories that are important to share with others. These are the stories that will help us move forward as an educational community.

We must remember to *always be brave* as we *face the sun and allow the shadows to fall behind us*. This means we have to *be a lamp, not a mirror* to uncover our stories and share our learning with others.

Some of the lessons in this book also remind us that the education profession is not perfect; *it is what it is* so we must *be the wave* and *bloom where we're planted* to survive sometimes. But if we *dream out loud* we have an opportunity to create our inspired future.

You will come to many crossroads on your path. You will make choices. When you see two roads diverge in front of you *follow your heart* and trust that the one you choose will lead you to where you need to be next. You know what it feels like when you make the right choice:

> Follow the bread crumbs that are put in front of you.
>
> Don't look back and second guess.
>
> Stay on course.
>
> As you take each step, *be a ripple*.
>
> And always remember to *pay it forward*.

APPENDIX A

AUTHORS WHO INSPIRE

As an avid reader I have books everywhere and I am often reading more than one book at a time. So it was difficult to narrow down my top 20 favorite authors for the section Learn About Influential Authors and Books. The authors in each of the chapters in many ways have served as mentors to me and have influenced my thinking at different points along my path. Their books are still on my shelves, and I consider each one a dear friend. Learn more about each author and think about the authors who have influenced you.

PRINTABLE REFLECTION QUESTIONS

The reflection questions that are presented throughout the book are provided on the companion website with space for your responses. Print them out and keep a record of your responses as you move through each lesson.

PRINTABLE POSTERS

THE TEN LESSONS

The opening page for each lesson, featuring Carol's original artwork, is available as a printable poster for your home or classroom.

TEN INSPIRING QUOTES

The inspiring quotes that close each lesson are also available to download on the companion website as printable posters.

PRINTABLE READING PLANS

The reading plans listed in Appendix B are available for download on the companion website. Take a look at the plans, and print out the one you choose to follow.

PODCAST INFORMATION

The podcast channel includes four podcasts that accompany each chapter:

- An introduction to each chapter's theme from Carol Radford
- An audio reading of Carol's story

- An interview with a teacher, who shares a story about a time in their career when they encountered that lesson

- An interview with an inspiring leader

The companion website at resources.corwin.com/TeachingWithLight also includes the following:

- A brief bio of each teacher who is interviewed on the podcast, *Another Teacher's Story*

- A brief bio of each inspiring leader who is interviewed on the podcast, *Listen to Inspiring Leaders.*

LEGACY TEACHER INTERVIEWS

We learn so much from the wisdom of others. This section of the companion website acknowledges several legacy teachers. Listen to their success stories to learn about their fulfilling careers in education. Reach out to retired teachers you know and thank them for their many contributions to education and students.

MINDFUL LIVING RESOURCES

Each lesson in this book lists resources and books that will support you in maintaining your balance. Links to each author's website are available in this section of the companion website.

MY WRITING JOURNEY

I am often asked how I got started writing books for teachers. This essay shares my writing process and journey over the years. I encourage teachers to write and share their ideas. I hope my journey inspires you to share what you know with others.

To access all of the above resources and more, visit resources.corwin.com/TeachingWithLight or scan the QR code below.

APPENDIX B

READING PLANS

In this section you will find reading plans for

These plans are also available on the companion website at Resources .Corwin.Com/TeachingWithLight.

PERSONAL REFLECTION AND INSPIRATION

Use this book as an opportunity to reflect on your journey so far and to think about your next steps. Look for themes and patterns that emerge from your reflections. You may complete the steps as you read the lessons or you may complete all your responses at the end of the book. Write your responses in a personal journal longhand, audio record your thoughts, or type your ideas on a device of your choice.

> **Step 1: Read** the Preface, Introduction, and Section I.
>
> **Write:**
>
> > a. Your reaction to these beginning ideas. What stands out to you as important?
> >
> > b. Is there anything new you didn't know or hadn't thought about before? List a few key ideas that you want to remember.
> >
> > c. Why did you decide to read this book? What did you hope to gain?
>
> **Step 2: Read** Lesson 1 Follow Your Heart.
>
> **Listen** to *Another Teacher's Story* podcast.
>
> **Write** your responses to the reflection questions listed under What's Your Story? Write longhand in your journal or type your responses.
>
> **Reflect** on what you wrote. What shows in your story that is meaningful to you right now? How does the message relate to a next step for you?
>
> **Step 3: Read** the other nine lessons or select those that are calling to you.
>
> **Listen** to *at least one* podcast from *Another Teacher's Story*.
>
> **Reflect** list at least three ideas you want to remember.
>
> **Step 4: Review** the Mindful Living Actions for the lessons you read.
>
> **Reflect** on the ideas of mindfulness, self-care, and your well-being.
>
> How will you use these ideas moving forward?
>
> **Take Action** and practice at least two practices from any of the lessons.
>
> **Step 5: Read** Section III Nurturing an Inspired Career
>
> **Assess** your career. What do you *wish* for? List three things that would support you. What are the *pluses* right now of being a teacher?

Additional activities: Review the authors, select one, and read a book; listen to at least one of the Inspired Leaders' podcasts; and explore Mindful Resources in each chapter.

TEACHER BOOK CLUBS

Invite teachers to read the book and reflect on their own journeys into teaching. Meetings can be virtual or in person. Limit the group size to five to eight teachers so there is an opportunity for everyone to share. Create more groups if there is more interest. Schedule professional development times to discuss the messages from the book or offer the club after-school hours. One teacher can facilitate the group and serve as the time keeper.

Prior to the meeting: A teacher volunteers to be the leader and sends an email inviting participants to read the Preface, Introduction, and Section I. Each person is encouraged to select one lesson from Section II and complete My Story reflections for that lesson.

Meeting Agenda: The teacher leader serves as the time keeper to ensure everyone has an opportunity to speak and share their story reflections. Each teacher shares the lesson they chose and why this expression was meaningful to them.

Other discussion options:

Mindful Living Actions: *Teachers share which ones they tried and how they worked.*

Be Inspired by the Words of Others: *Teachers share books or authors that stood out.*

Closing the meeting: Leader recites one of the quotes from one of the Feel Inspired lessons. Optional: Schedule another meeting. Select a new leader. Repeat agenda.

Do this as many times as the group would like to meet.

Closing the book club: When the group has decided how many times to meet the final meeting will include reading Section III and discussing the book as a whole.

Sample Questions:

What stands out as important to you in Section III of this book?

How did reading this book support your growth and development?

What did you learn about your colleagues at this book club meeting?

Is this the kind of professional learning that supports you? Explain.

Optional: Create an online evaluation for participants.

MENTOR/MENTEE PAIRS

A mentor and mentee read the book separately and come together to discuss key ideas. The option of writing reflections to any of the questions prior to meeting is encouraged but should not be required. The purpose of these meetings will be to use the lesson stories to share experiences beginning teachers may be facing, discuss healthy strategies for mindful living, and promote reading of inspirational books.

SAMPLE MEETING AGENDAS FOR MENTOR/MENTEE PAIRS

Meeting 1: (30min – 1hour) Reading the Preface, Introduction, and Section I.

Reflect: At the beginning of the meeting each person writes what stands out as the key ideas for this book.

Discuss and share other important ideas from Preface, Introduction and Section I that are most meaningful.

Meeting 2: (30min – 1hour) Read Lesson 1.

Bring written responses to Lesson 1's What's Your Story?

Share each person's journey into teaching.

Discuss: What did we learn about each other that we didn't know before?

Review Mindful Living Actions and Be Inspired by the Words of Others.

Meeting 3: (30min – 1hour) Select one other lesson to read and discuss.

Share and Discuss: Which lesson did you choose and why?

Review the Mindful Living Actions for each lesson and share your assessment from the lesson chapter.

Homework: Commit to practicing some healthy self-care.

Meeting 4: (30min – 1hour) Read Section III and star three ideas to discuss.

Write: Review the ideas you each starred, and write why they are so important to you at this time. Mentee shares first.

Share your intention for your teaching career and the three questions in Section III (what gives you joy).

Next Step: Share what this book has revealed as a next step.

Meeting 5: (30min – 1hour) Review the experience and share another lesson.

Discuss books and authors from the top-20 list.

Share inspiration from *Inspiring Leaders* podcasts

Reflect and summarize: How was this book useful to your growth? As a mentee? As a mentor?

Shared reading: Select a book to read together and discuss in the future.

TEACHER EDUCATION CANDIDATES

Use this book as a reflective process in any teacher preparation course or during the practicum experience. The purpose is to encourage candidates to be proactive in their thinking about the realities of teaching while using an inspirational format.

The goals for reading the book include (a) revealing inner wisdom through stories that relate to a pre-service teacher's journey into teaching, (b) an introduction to mindful practices to use in student teaching, and (c) an introduction to inspiring leaders and influential authors to ground teacher candidates' knowledge.

Invite the student teachers to read the book in sections. Limit the group size to five to eight teachers so there is an opportunity for everyone to share virtually or in person. One student teacher can facilitate the group and serve as the time keeper.

CLASS 1: READ THE PREFACE, INTRODUCTION, AND SECTION I

Write: List three important ideas that stand out to you, and share them in your group.

Create your Circle of Mentors (Section 1, page 11). Why are you selecting these people to support you?

Summarize: The group leader summarizes the key ideas from the discussion.

CLASS 2: READ LESSON 1 AND LISTEN TO THE PODCAST

Write your story: Read the My Story reflection prompts and write your responses.

Discuss the podcast and how it relates to anyone in the group.

Reflect: What did you learn about your classmates that you didn't already know?

CLASS 3: READ AT LEAST TWO OTHER LESSONS OF YOUR CHOICE

Share the two lessons you selected and why they stood out to you as important.

Discuss the Mindful Living Actions in any of the lessons shared.

Commit to practicing at least one action to promote your balance and well-being.

Reflect: Why is it important to focus on your social-emotional health as you enter teaching?

CLASS 4: READ SECTION III, REVIEW SECTION I, AND LISTEN TO ONE PODCAST

Share your intention for your teaching journey (page 10 refers to intention).

Discuss Inspired Leaders' podcasts.

Reflect: What are your responses to the Three Questions (page 10).

Summarize: What did you learn?

CLASS 5: READ INFLUENTIAL AUTHORS AND BOOKS (ALL LESSONS)

Discuss which two authors stand out as interesting to you. Why?

Read author bios in the Resources and share what you learned. Any surprises?

Optional Homework: Read one book from the Top 20 List.

Final Reflection: How has *Teaching With Light* helped you understand and prepare for becoming a teacher?

LEGACY TEACHERS

I am defining a *legacy teacher* as someone who has taught for more than 20 years and has much wisdom to still share. Pre-service teachers are beginning their careers, in-service teachers are actively in practice, and post-service teachers bring the legacy to our profession. Use this book as a way to reflect on your own experiences and think about how you might like to *pay it forward* to share your success stories with pre- and in-service teachers.

Read this book as a personal journey or find a few other retirees and read it together. Use this Reading Plan as a guide to your discussions. Select a group leader and a timekeeper to ensure everyone in the group has an opportunity to share.

SAMPLE MEETING AGENDAS FOR LEGACY TEACHERS

Prior to the launch meeting, read the Preface, Introduction, and Section I.

LAUNCH MEETING

1. Share why you are reading this book.

2. Discuss the concept of legacy teacher.

3. Each person shares one thing that stood out as important from the reading.

4. Set next meeting date.

5. Homework: Read Lessons 1–5 and listen to at least one podcast

NEXT MEETING

1. Discuss Lesson 1: Everyone shares their journey into teaching.

2. Discuss Lessons 2–5 with different people highlighting learning.

3. Share *Mindful Living Actions* and who tried what.

4. Which books have you read from *Be Inspired by the Words of Others?*

5. Next Meeting and Homework: Read Lessons 6–9 and listen to a podcast.

NEXT MEETING

1. Discuss Lessons 6–9: Different people selected different lessons.

2. Share *Mindful Living Actions* and who tried what.

3. Which books have you read from *Be Inspired by the Words of Others*?

4. Next Meeting and Homework: Listen to two Inspired Leaders' podcasts.

NEXT MEETING

1. Discuss podcasts: What did you learn?

2. Share Mindful Living Actions and who tried what.

3. Which books have you read from Be Inspired by the Words of Others?

4. Next Meeting and Homework: Read Lesson 10.

NEXT MEETING

1. Discuss Lesson 10: Pay it Forward.

2. Share: What gave you the most joy in your teaching career? Share that story.

3. What three pieces of practical advice would you share with a beginning teacher?

4. Next Meeting and Homework: Read Section III and Review Resources.

LAST MEETING

1. What stands out in Section III?

2. What will you do to *pay it forward*?

3. Discuss these ideas as potential actions to share your teacher wisdom. Select one!

ONE-TIME ACTIVITY

1. Share your practical advice with one real beginning teacher by phone.

2. Send a note to a beginning teacher(s) with encouraging ideas.

3. Be a guest speaker (video) at a school or in a teacher education course.

SOME LEVEL OF COMMITMENT

1. Create a blog or video to share your good ideas. Collaborate with others.

2. Volunteer in a novice teacher's classroom (virtual helper or in person).

3. Teach or co-teach a practical course in teacher education.

DEEP COMMITMENT

1. Reach out to your own district, and offer to volunteer to be part of sustaining the district's mentoring program. Collaborate with and mentor up-and-coming mentor leaders.

2. Organize a group of retirees to support novice teachers in their classrooms.

3. Create a legacy program in your school with retirees contributing to committees and mentoring programs.

4. Write your own book with your wisdom and stories.

5. Collaborate on teaching research with a higher education professor.

6. Serve on a state committee for teachers or public policy reviews.

7. Join a professional organization and share your wisdom.

8. Serve on a school board.

9. Collaborate with a business to bring scholarships to teachers for inspired personal development.

10. Create an awards ceremony to honor the legacy of retired teachers.

Create your own pay-it-forward ideas.

REFERENCES

Ainsworth, L. (n.d.). "I touch the future; I teach": Teaching as selfless service. https://corwin-connect.com/2018/09/i-touch-the-future-i-teach-teaching-as-selfless-service/

Barth, R. S. (1990). *Improving schools from within: Teachers, parents, and principals can make the difference.* Jossey-Bass.

Brown, B. (2015). *Daring greatly: How the courage to be vulnerable transforms the way we live, love, parent, and lead.* Penguin.

Buttenheim, M. N. (2016). *Expanding joy: Let your yoga dance. Embodying positive psychology.* Grace in Motion. https://www.letyouryogadance.com/

Campbell, J. (1999). *The hero's journey: Joseph Campbell on his life and work.* Harper & Row.

Cameron, J. (2016). *The artist's way: A spiritual path to higher creativity (25th anniversary edition).* Tarcher Perigee.

Chand, J. (n.d.). Qigong for vitality. https://www.qigongforvitality.com/about/

Chödrön, P. (2001). *Start where you are: A guide to compassionate living.* Shambhala.

Clark, M. (n.d.). Facilitating personal and spiritual development. https://www.inspiredideas.me/

Collins, T. (1999). *The Western guide to feng shui: Room by room.* Hay House.

Duarte, N. (2010). *Resonate: Present visual stories that transform audiences.* John Wiley and Sons.

Dyer, W. (2009). *Change your thoughts—change your life: Living the wisdom of the Tao.* Hay House.

Frost, R. (1916, January 1). "The road not taken," *Mountain Interval.* Henry Holt.

Fullan, M., & Hargreaves, A. (1991). *What's worth fighting for? Working together for your school.*

Gabai, N. (n.d.). Innovative solutions for your home and office. http://www.b-organized.net/

Gabel, M., & Walker, J. (2006, September-October). The anticipatory leader: Buckminster Fuller's principles for making the world work. *The Futurist.* http://www.wfs.org

Gawain, S. (2016). *Creative visualization: Use the power of your imagination to create what you want in your life.* Nataraj.

Gilbert, E. (2015). *Big magic: Creative living beyond fear.* Riverhead Books.

Gobin, R. (2019). *The self-care prescription: Powerful solutions to manage stress, reduce anxiety and increase well-being.* Althea Press.

Greenberg, M. T., Brown J. L., & Abenavoli, R. M. (2016, September). *Teacher stress and health: Effects on teachers, students, and schools.* Edna Bennett Pierce Prevention Research Center, Pennsylvania State University. https://review.prevention.psu.edu/uploads/files/rwjf430428-TeacherStress.pdf

Hạnh, T. N. (2014). *How to EAT.* Parallax Press.

Hạnh, T. N. (1997). *True love: A practice of awakening the heart.* Shambala.

Hạnh, T. N. (1987). *The Miracle of mindfulness.* Beacon Press.

Hargreaves, A., & Fink, D. (2006). *Sustainable leadership.* Jossey Bass.

Hargreaves, A., & O'Connor, M. T. (2018, May). *Collaborative professionalism: When teaching together means learning for all.* Corwin.

Heider, J. (2014). *The Tao of leadership: Lao Tzu's Tao Te Ching adapted for a new age.* Humanics New Age.

Himes, M. (2010, February). *On discernment: Three questions.* Visitation Monastery of Minneapolis. https://www.visitationmonasteryminneapolis.org/2010/02/on-discernment-three-key-questions/

Hodel, P. (2009). *Monday hearts for Madalene.* Stewart, Tabori, and Chang.

Hough, L. (2020, Summer). PD also means personal development: Ed.L.D. student creates development program for new teachers to manage stress and well-being. *Harvard Ed. Magazine.* https://www.gse.harvard.edu/news/ed/20/05/pd-also-means-personal-development

Intrator, S. M. (2002). *Stories of the courage to teach: Honoring the teacher's heart.* Jossey-Bass.

Intrator, S. M. & Scribner, M. (2003). *Teaching with fire: Poetry that sustains the courage to teach.* Jossey-Bass.

Intrator, S. M., & Scribner, M. (2014). *Teaching with heart: Poetry that speaks to the courage to teach.* Jossey-Bass.

James, J. (1986). *Success is the quality of your journey.* Newmarket Press.

Jennings, S., & Kenneally, G. (2015). *The lotus kitchen.* Huqua Press.

Johnson, S. M. (2004). *Finders and keepers: Helping new teachers survive and thrive in our schools.* Jossey-Bass.

Johnson, S. M. (2019). *Where teachers thrive: Organizing schools for success.* Harvard Education Press.

Jones, S., Bouffard S. M., & Weissbourd, R. (2013, May). *Educators' social and emotional skills vital to learning.* Kappan. http://www.nationalresilienceresource.com/Education/Educators_social_and_emotional_skills.pdf

Jordan, J. (1980, October 1). "Poem for South African women." *Passion: New poems, 1977–1980.* Beacon Press.

Kabat-Zinn, J. (1994). *Wherever you go, there you are: Mindfulness meditation in everyday life.* Hyperion.

Kegan, R., & Lahey, L. L. (2009). *Immunity to change: How to overcome it and unlock potential in yourself and your organization.* Harvard Business Press. https://mindsatwork.com/who-we-are/

Kingston, K. (1999). *Clear your clutter with feng shui: Free yourself from physical, mental, emotional, and spiritual clutter forever.* Harmony Books.

Kovanda, D. (n.d.) Kind yoga is for everyone. https://kindyoga.com/

Kovanda, D., & Gamble, A. (2016). *Good night yoga.* Good Night Books. https://kindyoga.com/

Kowalski, K. (n.d.). "Call me Trim Tab" — Buckminster Fuller and the impact of an individual on society. https://www.sloww.co/trim-tab-buckminster-fuller/

Lee, K. (2014). *Reset: Make the most of your stress. Your 24-7 plan for well-being.* iUniverse.

Lee, K. (2018). *Mentalligence: A new psychology of thinking—learn what it takes to be more agile, mindful, and connected in today's world.* Health Communications.

Li, Q. (2018). *Forest bathing: How trees can help you find health and happiness.* Penguin.

Lin, C. (n.d.). Qigong healing connection. https://www.springforestqigong.com/

Linn, D., & Linn, M. (2012). *The mystic cookbook: The secret alchemy of food.* Hay House.

Maeroff, G. I. (1988, March 23). The empowerment of teachers. *Education Week.* https://www.edweek.org/ew/articles/1988/03/23/26maer.h07.html

Marzelli, C. (n.d.). Be still and know. http://www.stillwoman.com/

McGonigal, K. (2016). *The upside of stress: Why stress is good for you, and how to get good at it.* Penguin.

Meriam-Webster. (n.d.). Change. Retrieved November 20, 2020, from https://www.merriam-webster.com/dictionary/change

Murray, E. (2014). *Living life in full bloom: 120 daily practices to deepen your passion, creativity and relationships.* Rodale Books.

Nieto, S. (2003). *What keeps teachers going?* Teachers College Press.

Oliver, M. (1992). "The Summer Day." *New and selected poems by Mary Oliver.* Beacon Press.

Olson, K., & Brown, V. (2015). *The mindful school leader: Practices to transform your leadership and school.* Corwin.

Palmer, P. J. (2000). *Let your life speak: Listening for the voice of vocation.* Jossey-Bass.

Palmer, P. J. (2018). *On the brink of everything: Grace, gravity, and getting old.* Berrett-Koehler Publishers.

Palmer, P. J. (1998). *The courage to teach: Exploring the inner landscape of a teacher's life.* Jossey-Bass.

Plevin, J. (2019). *The healing magic of forest bathing: Finding calm, creativity, and connection in the natural world.* Ten Speed Press.

Radford, C. P. (2019). *A mindful living journal: Art and affirmations to nourish your soul.* Nellies Notecards.

Radford, C. P. (2019). *Mindful mentoring: A reflective guide for mentors and mentees.* Bowker Identifier Services.

Roberts, A., & Kim, H. (2019, May 6). To promote success in schools, focus on teacher well-being. *Education Plus Development.* https://www.brookings.edu/blog/education-plus-development/2019/05/06/to-promote-success-in-schools-focus-on-teacher-well-being/

Ruiz, D. M. (1997). *The four agreements.* Amber-Allen.

Samuels, M., & Lane, M. R. (2013). *Healing with the arts: A 12-week program to heal yourself and your community.* Simon and Schuster.

Saradananda, S. (2015). *Mudras for modern life: Boost your health, re-energize your life, enhance your yoga and deepen your meditation.* Watkins.

Schildkret, D. (2018). *Morning altars: A 7-step practice to nourish your spirit through nature, art, and ritual.* Countryman Press.

Smith, T., & Waller, J. (2019). *Ridiculously amazing schools: Creating a culture where everyone thrives.* Publish Your Purpose Press.

Sweet Honey in the Rock. (1998). We are the ones [Song]. On . . . *Twenty Five . . . .* Ryko/Rhino.

Taylor, M. (2008). *DailyOM: Inspirational thoughts for a happy, healthy, and fulfilling day.* Hay House. https://www.dailyom.com/

Williamson, M. (1993, March 15). "Our deepest fear." *A return to love.* HarperOne.

A SAGE Publishing Company

Helping educators make the greatest impact

CORWIN HAS ONE MISSION: to enhance education through intentional professional learning.

We build long-term relationships with our authors, educators, clients, and associations who partner with us to develop and continuously improve the best evidence-based practices that establish and support lifelong learning.